You, Your Family & the Law

A Legal Guide for Today's Families

Author: Wesley J. Smith
Editor: Kay Ostberg
Project Director: Theresa Meehan Rudy
Graphics & Production: David Bell
Substantial Assistance Provided By: Allysa Jang, Katherine J. Lee and
Caleen Norrod

Our thanks to the following consumer specialists and attorneys for their
invaluable comments and advice: Gerri Detweiler, Richard Eisen, James E.
Jeffries, Heather Hyde, Janet Mahoney, Leslye Orloff, Janice Presser and
Mark Rosenberg.

First Edition: October, 1993

ISBN 0-910073-18-X

TABLE OF
CONTENTS

PART 4   OTHER FAMILY ISSUES

APPENDICES

INTRODUCTION

Families, like the rest of society, are increasingly finding themselves caught-up in the growing complexity of modern life. Everything has become so fast-paced, so complicated and perhaps worst of all, so legalistic. It seems that every time a family turns around, they are faced with issues or decisions that involve the law.

The law governs most of our most intimate relationships: marriage, having children, getting divorced, living together. But family law can be viewed as much more than these traditional topics. How families relate with society and make business decisions, such as purchasing insurance or buying a house, also have a large impact on the quality of our lives and the future of our families. For that reason, this book has touched on some issues that are not usually thought of when the subject of family law is addressed.

A WORD ABOUT TERMS

You don't need a law degree to use this book and understand its contents. Yet, a discussion of matters legalistic must invariably use legal words and phrases that lawyers call "words of art." In the field of family law, words such as paternity, annulment, prenuptial agreement, custody and decree are but just a few of the legal terms you'll encounter. Every time a new legal term or phrased is used in this book, it is printed in italics. A definition of the word appears in the text with the legal term, and in the Glossary (Appendix 3) at the end of the book.

HOW TO USE THIS BOOK

This book's principal value to you will be as a resource in time of need. You can flip to the section of the book that deals with your area of concern. For example, if you are involved in a divorce and want to find out if there is a way to achieve a fair and peaceful settlement, you will want to turn to Part 3 and read Chapter 7. Or, suppose you want to adopt a stepchild and wonder if you need the consent of a natural parent who hasn't been heard from for three years; Chapter 5, found in Part 2, will tell you about the law of abandonment as it affects adoption.

DEALING WITH PROFESSIONALS

Although this book gives a general description of the law; it cannot give you legal or tax advice based on your individual circumstances. However, most of the time, the information you receive in these pages should be sufficient for you to understand your rights, or at least the issues you need to research further. Problem areas are flagged where you may need professional advice or assistance. You may also wish to conduct further research (see the Bibliography, Appendix 4) or contact an organization that provides information or assistance on the topic of interest to you (see National Organizations, Appendix 5).

PART 1

GETTING MARRIED

1

HOW MARRIAGE IS CREATED

Marriage is more than a loving relationship between two people that hopefully (but not inevitably) lasts a lifetime. It is a legal status, governed by law.

Most of the laws concerning marriage in the United States have their roots in feudal England, where marriage was a religious event—holy matrimony—that served as a sanction for sexual relationships, the bearing of children and the creation of a familial relationship between a man and a woman. The rules and guidelines that controlled the relationship were provided by church law and enforced by ecclesiastical (church) courts. "Informal" marriages were also allowed in "jolly olde England," which have their counterparts in the "common law" marriages valid in a few states in this country to this very day.

Unlike England, in the United States, marriage has always been under the control of the government. However, with that exception, many of the laws governing marriage in both nations were the same. When a man and a woman married, they became one person under the law—and that person was the man. A married woman had the right to her husband's support but other than that, the man was in charge. He held the property. He had the legal right to control his wife's behavior and any property she may have brought into the marriage. He also had the right to sexual relations, whether his wife was "in the mood" or not. Indeed, until modern times, a man could not be charged with the crime of raping his wife.

In recent years the law of marriage has evolved at an almost dizzying pace. Women own their own property, control their finances and choose where they want to live—whether or not it is with their husband. A woman may now refuse sex with her husband, who may be guilty of the crime of rape if he forces the issue. The laws governing intimate relations are expanding, with many rights and incidents of marriage available to people who live together in an intimate relationship (known as *cohabitation*) without being legally married.

This chapter will introduce the topic of modern marriage. Among the topics to be discussed are: Who may marry? How is a marriage created? When is a marriage legally binding? Does the law recognize "common law" marriage? Are marriages made in a different state or in a foreign country legal throughout the United States?

QUESTIONS ABOUT MARRIAGE

What Is a Marriage?

Religious issues aside, a marriage is a government-sanctioned bond freely entered into between a man and a woman who agree to be joined together as husband and wife. The power to regulate marriage rests with each state, which establishes through its laws who can marry, under what conditions, and the rights and obligations of the parties to each other.

What Are the Formal Requirements for a Marriage?

There are three requirements to be met before a marriage is legally created: consent, the legal ability to marry and participation in a ceremony with a license (known as *solemnization*).

Consent. To be valid, a marriage requires the free and voluntary consent of both the woman and the man.

The Legal Ability to Marry. Not everyone can legally give their consent to marry. Any "marriage" that people who cannot under the law consent to marry try to create will not be recognized as valid by the state. These include:

Minors. A person under the age of 18 must usually have permission from a parent or guardian to legally marry. This provision does not apply to minors who are *emancipated* (living free and independently) from their parents care and control.

The mentally retarded. People who are legally considered mentally disabled may not have the capacity to marry *if* they cannot understand the nature and consequences of their decision.

People who are already married. If someone is legally married, he or she may not consent to remarry until the prior marriage is legally terminated.

Homosexuals. Gay men and lesbians may not enter same-sex marriages.

People who are related by blood. The existence of this prohibition depends on how close the relationship is. Marriages within the immediate family—i.e., parents and children, brothers and sisters—are prohibited in every state. Most states prohibit marriages between an uncle and a niece or an aunt and a nephew. Approximately one-half of the states prohibit marriages between first cousins. Most states also prohibit marriage between people related by adoption and many prohibit step-parent/child marriages, although the number is decreasing.

If people who cannot legally consent to marry do so, the "marriage" will not be recognized under the law and neither person will be considered married. These marriages are known as *void marriages* and do not require a court ruling to end them.

There are also times where the consent of one of the parties has been obtained under circumstances where the law will permit the person to take back their consent and obtain a court ruling that the marriage never existed (*annulment*). These are known in the law as *voidable marriages.* Voidable marriages require a court order to invalidate the union. Voidable marriages include situations where:

Consent was obtained through fraud. Fraud exists where one party was persuaded to consent to marriage based on false statements or promises. In order for there to be grounds for an annulment, the false statement must have been a significant inducement to the consent. For example, if a man tells his prospective wife he wants to be the father of her children when he knows he is sterile, and the woman consents to the marriage relying on the representation, she would have been the victim of fraud and could probably obtain an annulment.

Consent obtained through duress. If someone marries because of a serious threat, the marriage may be voidable. A woman who is forced (through psychological, emotional or physical pressure) to marry because she is pregnant might later be allowed to obtain an annulment because her consent was obtained under duress.

Impediments to marriage. There are certain circumstances that will permit an annulment, even when both the parties acted in good faith. For example, if a man is impotent at the time of marriage thereby preventing consummation, that may allow the wife to annul the union. However, if the impotence develops after consummation, that would not be grounds for an annulment.

Marriage entered in jest. If people enter a mock marriage with no intention to be bound, the marriage is voidable.

Sham marriages. If people marry with an ulterior motive, the marriage may be voidable. In some cases, the government may refuse to recognize such marriages. A typical example is a marriage entered between a U.S. citizen and a noncitizen with the sole purpose of using the marriage to gain the noncitizen legal entry into the country.

In order to obtain an annulment, the party who wishes to terminate the marriage must act quickly upon learning the facts which caused the faulty consent. Otherwise, the marriage may be considered valid. Thus, the woman whose future husband told her he wanted to father her children, knowing he was sterile, will not be allowed to annul the marriage if she remains with him after discovering the truth.

Ceremony With a License. In most cases, to be legal a marriage must be performed by someone legally sanctioned to perform the marriage and documented with a license (*solemnized*). There are several purposes for requiring solemnization:

- To impress upon the engaged couple the importance of what they are about to do.
- To create a permanent record of the marriage.
- To give the public notice of the marriage.
- To collect vital statistics.

To marry, you need to get a marriage license, have a ceremony, and complete the post-ceremony red tape.

The license. The rules that govern marriage licenses are governed by the law of each state. Most require blood tests to check for venereal disease. Some states also test for other problems, such as blood Rh compatibility, and several states require HIV tests to check for the virus that causes AIDS.

The ceremony. The marriage ceremony must be performed by a person, such as an ordained minister, priest or judge, who is legally empowered to marry people. The ceremony must also be witnessed, usually by a minimum of two people. At the ceremony, the marrying couple must publicly state they wish to marry.

The red tape. After the marriage ceremony, the presiding minister or judge must complete the marriage license, stating the place and date of marriage, and must send it to the county recorder or other appropriate state agency for recording as a public record.

Must a Marriage Be Consummated to Be Legally Valid?

Generally, a marriage is legal once it has been performed. However, failure to engage in sexual intercourse (consummate the marriage) may provide grounds for a later annulment. Consummation may be required to create a common law marriage.

What Is a Common Law Marriage?

A common law marriage is one that is created without the legal ceremony or license. While the exact rules differ among the states that legally recognize common law marriages, most states require that the parties agree to be husband and wife, that the "marriage" be consummated and that the pair hold themselves out to the world as a married couple. The marriage takes place upon the agreement to be married and the consummation. Once the consummation has occurred based on the agreement, the marriage exists. Thirteen states (Alabama, Colorado, Georgia, Idaho, Iowa, Kansas, Montana, Ohio, Oklahoma, Pennsylvania, Rhode Island, South Carolina and Texas) and the District of Columbia recognize common law marriage. The other states do not allow common law marriages.

What Law Governs a Marriage?

The laws that govern marriage are controlled by each of the states. (Federal law may apply to the marriage, such as in the areas of taxation, Social Security and other government programs.)

The Law That Decides Whether a Marriage Is Valid. Generally, a marriage that is valid where it is created is legal in every state and is binding on the federal government—even if the marriage took place in another country. This is true even if the marriage was created in a way that is not valid throughout the country. For example, California does not allow its citizens to create a common law marriage but will recognize a marriage so created in a state where such unions are legal.

> Texans Mary and Johnny were in love. They decided to marry. They held each other's hand, both said, "I marry thee," and then they went on a romantic honeymoon where they consummated their "marriage." After that, they lived together, told their friends and neighbors that they were married and wore wedding rings. Under Texas law, they had a valid common law marriage.
> Later, they moved to Illinois, a state which does not allow common law marriages. There, they broke up. Mary wanted a divorce and the right to her marital share of the property. Johnny said that they were never married since there had been no ceremony or license and thus, there could be no divorce.
> The case went to court where Mary won. The court ruled that since the marriage was valid in Texas, it was valid in Illinois. Thus, even though the state where the couple then lived did not allow its residents to create a common law marriage, the law recognized Mary and Johnny's marriage because it was legal and valid in the state where it was created.

The Laws That Apply During the Marriage. The law of a state in which a married couple resides generally control the rules of their relationship, even if they were married in a different state with different laws.

> Paul and Linda were married in California, a state where property obtained during the marriage is owned equally by the parties and each have a right to an equal share of the property if they divorce. Soon thereafter, they moved to New York, a state with different property laws, which permits an unequal division of property acquired during marriage upon divorce. If the couple divorced while living in New York, the laws of New York would apply and not the laws of California, even though they were married in California.

What If Someone Believes They're Married But They're Not?

A favorite situation comedy plot is for a happily married couple to discover that their marriage license was invalid or the minister who performed the ceremony was a fraud. That means they are not legally married. What are they to do?

Show business aside, such mistakes occasionally happen in real life, and the law has rules to protect the parties who have acted in good faith. If a person believes he or she is legally married, the law will recognized him or her as married. For example, if Mary married Johnny in a ceremony with a license but did not know that he had a wife whom he had never divorced, she would not be legally married. However, she could have the same rights as a married person despite this fact and her rights would continue to accrue as if she were legally married until she discovered the problem. Thus, Mary would enjoy the same property rights, the right to support and other rights as a married woman until she discovered that her "marriage" was not valid.

(People who know they are not legally married do not have this protection.)

Once legally married, spouses have rights and duties that they owe to and receive from each other. They also have rights and obligations to third parties, such as the government and creditors. These topics are the subject of the next chapter.

2

THE RIGHTS & RESPONSIBILITIES OF SPOUSES

Once a man and a woman marry, their legal relation with each other and with the outside world changes. The legal status of marriage creates specific and enforceable rights and responsibilities. Some of these exist between the parties to the marriage while others exist between the married couple and the outside world. This chapter will describe the most important of these rights and responsibilities, including the property rights of married people, special laws that apply to married people and the duties married people owe each other.

PROPERTY RIGHTS AND MARRIED PEOPLE

Generally, there are two types of laws utilized by the different states to govern the manner in which married people own property: *separate property* laws and *community property* laws. The distinction is important during the marriage because the laws determine which spouse has the power to manage and control property obtained during the marriage. This distinction used to be important in divorce law, but as Chapter 7 will describe, the distinction between separate property states and community property states is now far less important.

Separate Property States

In states with separate property laws, both the husband and the wife enjoy sole ownership of property that is held in their individual name—even if the property is obtained during the marriage. Thus, if you use your salary to buy a condominium and you put it in your name alone, it is owned by you as your separate property—even though the property was obtained during marriage from funds earned during the marriage.

This does not mean that spouses must hold property under separate ownership. A couple, whether legally married or not, can agree to hold property as co-owners. For example, the property can be held together as *joint tenants,* in *tenancy by the entirety,* or as *tenants in common.*

Joint Tenancy. If property is held in joint tenancy, both husband and wife own what is known as an undivided interest in the whole. That means both own the whole thing. That also means that both have an equal right to manage and control the property. Thus, if one party wants to sell the property and the other does not, it might take court action to force the sale. Joint tenancy also has the *right of survivorship.* A right of survivorship means that if one of the joint tenants dies, the other joint tenant becomes the sole owner of the entire property as a matter of law immediately upon the death.

Tenancy By the Entirety. A few states have a special ownership arrangement just for married couples called tenancy by the entirety. It's like a joint tenancy except that the property owners must be married and their joint ownership can only be broken by a dissolution of the marriage. (That is not true of a joint tenancy.) The right of survivorship always applies.

Tenancy in Common. Tenancy in common basically means that each spouse (or tenant) owns one half of the property— although different percentages can be agreed upon. There is no right of survivorship. Thus, if one owner dies, his or her percentage of ownership will be transferred to heirs or those named in a will, rather than the other owners.

If a couple elects to co-own property, it's presumed that the person who paid for the property intends that the other receive a gift of the interest they are given in the property. However, in some states, if it was the wife who purchased the property, the presumption that she intended to give her husband an interest in the property does not apply.

In separate property states, property acquired during the marriage and held in the name of one of the spouses may be subject to division between the parties in a divorce if it was obtained during the marriage. Property division will be discussed in Chapter 8.

Despite the fact that property can be held separately, the laws of separate property states protect married partners in the event of the death of their spouse. Upon the death of its owner, property held separately is passed by will or by the laws of inheritance if there is no will. However, if a spouse is not provided for in a will, or is dissatisfied with the will's provisions, he or she may "elect" to take a "statutory share" of their spouse's property rather than the amount provided for them in the will. Most states allow the spouse to take one-third of the estate. This right exists regardless of the content of the will.

If there is no will, the laws of the state will prescribe how the property is passed to heirs. A spouse will generally take all of the property if there are no children or if the person who died had no living parents. If there are children or living parents, the spouse's share will be reduced but generally not to lower than one-third.

Community Property States

Eight states (Arizona, California, Idaho, Louisiana, New Mexico, Nevada, Texas, and Washington) have a different approach to the property of married people. This law, which is based on the Spanish rather than the English model, is called community property.

In a community property state, property acquired during the marriage is owned equally by the husband and the wife. Thus, even if the husband works and the wife stays home, property purchased with the husband's earnings is one-half owned by the wife. This includes the right to pensions, bank accounts, real estate, furnishings, automobiles and other assets.

Of course, nothing in law is simple. To say that each spouse is an equal does not tell the full story. There are exceptions that you must be aware of if you are to understand the law of community property:

Separate Property Rights. Married people who live in community property states can still own property in their own name, even if it is obtained during a marriage. Separate property of a married person includes property owned before the marriage, property obtained by gift or inheritance during a marriage, and property the married couple agrees by contract will be owned by one of them as sole and separate. The owner of separate property has the right to exclusive use and control of the property and may do with it whatever he or she wishes without the other spouse's permission.

Management and Control. At one time, the husband had the right to manage and control community property, even though the wife was an equal owner. This is no longer true. Under current law, if you live in a community property state, you generally have an equal right to control the property and your permission must be obtained by your spouse if he or she wishes to sell, give away or otherwise dispose of property. However, Texas has a rule allowing the spouse who would have had control over the property, if it had been obtained while single, to control property even though it is community in nature. Thus, as to the issue of management and control, Texas law is equivalent to a separate property state.

If Your Spouse Dies

If your spouse dies, you automatically own one-half of all community property. That being so, the law does not provide a spousal election to invalidate the provisions of a will as is done in separate property states. Thus, your spouse can leave his or her one-half of the community property and all separate property, to whomever and however he or she wishes.

If your spouse dies without a will, you keep your half of the community property; and your spouse's half—along with his or her separate property—will be divided among you, your children and/or your dead spouse's parents, as provided by law. Your share of your spouse's separate property and one-half share of the community property will not be less than one-third. However, a spouse can be disinherited from receiving a share of separate property in a will.

Property Can Be Held Jointly

Community property states also permit married couples to hold title to property as joint tenants or tenants in common, with the same rules applying as exist in separate property states.

In the Event of a Divorce

A community property state divides all community property equally between the divorcing husband and wife. This can be more complicated than it may sound. The issue of property division in community property states will be detailed in Chapter 8.

Lisa and Eddie were married in a separate property state. Lisa was a business executive, earning a large salary. She purchased a condominium with her salary and held title in her own name. When she decided to sell it, Eddie objected. He liked the condo and wanted to keep it in the family. Lisa would be able to sell the property despite the objections of her husband (assuming they did not divorce).

Later, Lisa died. When she died, she owned a house worth $150,000 and stock worth $150,000 which she had inherited from her mother. Lisa had excluded her husband from the will and left all of the property to her children from a prior marriage. Eddie elected to enforce his right to receive a statutory share of his deceased wife's property. The probate court agreed that he had the right to $100,000—⅓ of all of his deceased wife's property. The children received the remaining $200,000.

Jim and Lily were also married. They lived in a community property state. Jim earned a large salary and used the money he earned to purchase a condominium. Later, he wanted to sell it and Lily objected. The sale could not be completed because under the law, Lily owned half the property even though her name was not on the title to the property.

Later, Jim died and left all of his property to his children from a former marriage in his will. His property consisted of a house worth $150,000, which was in his name but was community property, and stocks worth $150,000 that he had inherited from his mother. Lily sought her share of the

(Continued)

property of her dead husband. She was able to receive $75,000—one half of the community property house—but received nothing from the stocks which had been her husband's separate property, because he had disinherited her. (If her husband had died without a will, she would have received no less than one-third of her husband's separate property, no less than one-third of her husband's portion of the community property and all of her share of the community property.)

SPECIAL LAWS THAT APPLY TO MARRIED COUPLES

The fact that a man and woman become husband and wife gives them added rights under the law that they would not otherwise have. Among the most notable of these are the following:

You Cannot Be Forced to Testify Against Your Spouse

The public policy in this nation is to support the stability of marriages. One of the ways the government has done this has been to create a special rule in the law of evidence that protects a spouse from being compelled to testify against his or her marriage partner. This applies even in criminal cases. The rationale is that confidential communication between spouses must be protected. That is not to say that a spouse cannot testify but that he or she cannot be *forced* to testify.

You Can Sue for Loss of Consortium or Wrongful Death

If your spouse is injured or killed because of the negligence or intentional actions of another, you can sue for your losses, even if you were not involved in the accident. One of the losses you can collect money for is what is known in the law as *the loss of consortium*. That means, if you lose companionship and services, including sexual relations, because of your spouse's injury or death, you have the right to collect money damages.

You can also collect for *wrongful death* if your husband or wife is killed. The amount of money you get is generally determined by the financial cost of your spouse's death to you and your family. Thus, if two people are killed at a crosswalk when a drunk driver runs a red light, and one is employed and earns a large salary and the other is a street person, the damages collected by the spouse of the person who earned high wages would probably be much higher than the damages collected by the spouse of the street person who was not working. (Wrongful death suits can also be brought by children and parents.)

You May Not Be Able to Sue Your Spouse

At one time, a husband or wife could not sue each other for torts. (A tort is a civil wrong that gives the victim the right to damages.) This prohibition was known as *interspousal immunity*.

Today, most states' spousal immunity laws have been eliminated or substantially weakened. However, many liability insurance policies will not pay benefits for interfamily lawsuits. (This is sometimes known as the "family exclusion clause" and covers family members who live in the same household.) Thus, if a husband causes an automobile accident injuring his wife, the auto insurance company will not have to pay under the liability section of the policy if she brings a lawsuit against him. (The company may have to pay under other parts of the insurance policy, such as medical pay provisions.)

A Wife Has a Choice of Last Names

When a woman marries, she can keep her last name, adopt a hyphenated last name of her and her husband's last names, or adopt her husband's last name. Any of these can be done without a formal court order. Although a man is less likely to do so, he may adopt a hyphenated last name of his and his wife's last name, or adopt his wife's last name upon marriage.

Preventing Abuse

At one time, a husband could not be guilty of raping his wife, nor would the law usually intervene in troubled marriages to prevent physical abuse. Today, that is changing. Police are increasingly being trained to protect battered spouses who can find assistance from the law against abuse if they are willing to assert their rights. For more details, see Chapter 11.

The Tax Consequences of Being Married

Income taxing entities treat married taxpayers differently from single taxpayers. Thus, a married couple is allowed to file a joint return, which can save them money if they are living on one income, while an unmarried couple living together are not able to file a joint return. On the other hand, if you're part of a married two-income household, your taxes may be higher because the I.R.S. will charge you a higher tax rate as a married taxpayer on your total earnings than it would if you were single. Thus, if you earn $40,000 in taxable income and your spouse earns $40,000, the total tax bite paid on the $80,000 joint income will be higher than the total amount paid by two single people earning $40,000 each. If you file a separate return when you are married, your tax will be higher than a single person's with the same income (all other things being equal). This is known as the "marriage penalty." The more money each spouse earns, the stiffer the marriage penalty.

Government Benefits

Your status as a married person can help you when it comes to qualifying for government benefits. Take Social Security for example. If you're a stay-at-home spouse and your husband or wife works, you are earning credits toward Social Security and Medicare qualification, even though you have no personal earnings. (To qualify for Social Security benefits, you have to earn work credits.) If you are married for ten years, you can qualify for Social Security Retirement benefits and Medicare, even if your spouse has died or you have divorced by the time you apply for benefits. (Your status as a spouse may also give you the right to Social Security survivor benefits, dependent benefits and Veterans' benefits.[*])

THE DUTIES THAT MARRIED PEOPLE OWE EACH OTHER

Many of the duties that married people owe each other exist during marriage. Others only arise if the couple separates or

---

* See HALT's book, *Legal Rights for Seniors: A Guide to Health Care, Income Benefits and Senior Legal Services*, for details.)

divorces. Here is a description of the most important of these rights:

The Mutual Obligation of Support

In most states, husbands and wives owe each other the mutual obligation of support during their marriage and this duty applies equally to both. (Under former law, the responsibility was solely the man's.)

What does this mean? Upon a divorce, it may mean that the court could order one party to pay the other *alimony*. (The topic of alimony will be discussed in Chapter 8.) But spouses also have a support obligation during a marriage. They include:

Providing for "Necessaries." Traditionally, the legal obligation of support during the ongoing marriage extended only to "necessaries." Here's how it works: If someone supplied your spouse a necessity such as food, medical care, transportation or housing, that person could hold you legally responsible for the cost.

An Obligation to Support the Family. Some states (California, Colorado, Connecticut, Illinois, Iowa, Massachusetts, Minnesota, Nebraska, North Dakota, Oregon, South Dakota, Utah, West Virginia, Wyoming) have passed laws which state that the expenses incurred providing for the family, including children, are chargeable against the property of either the husband or wife, or of them both. These are known as family support statutes. Thus, if a doctor provides emergency medical care for your spouse, you could be forced to pay the price of the care from your separate property.

The Right to Act on Behalf of Your Husband or Wife

Some states allow a husband or wife to act legally for the other (be each other's agent). An *agency* is created when one person acts at the request and on the behalf of another. For example, if Henry asked Sally to pick up a television, and the television store allowed Sally to take it on behalf of Henry, Henry could be held responsible for the cost of the TV even though it was picked up by Sally.

Most of the time the exercise of these legal rights never result in court action.

The Responsibility to Pay Debts in Community Property States

As explained earlier, some states are community property states. In a community property state, debts incurred during a marriage are generally the responsibility of both the husband and the wife. This obligation can be enforced against them as a couple and/or against either as an individual. Thus, if a husband incurs a $5,000 debt on a credit card during the marriage and defaults on the debt, the wife may be forced to pay the bill even though her name is not on the card.

Sexual Fidelity

One of the primary emotional benefits most people seek when they marry is the mutually monogamous sexual relationship that is an important part of the social contract of marriage. At one time, breaching that social contract was a serious issue for the law. Indeed, in many states, *adultery* (the sexual intercourse of a married individual with someone other than their spouse) used to be a criminal offense, not to mention a ground for divorce. (Adultery remains a ground for divorce in 28 states but most states allow divorce regardless of fault. See Chapter 7.) Today, few states have laws criminalizing adultery and those that do rarely, if ever, enforce them.

The Right to Privacy

The law recognizes the right of married couples to make intimate decisions about their life without interference from the government. For example, the government cannot prevent you from using birth control or other family planning procedures, including abortion. Laws that used to criminalize certain sexual practices, such as oral or anal intercourse (known as sodomy statutes), have also been removed from the books in many states. Twenty-eight states still have sodomy statutes on the books, generally using them to prosecute gay men. Still, in states where sodomy laws remain on the books, there is nothing preventing these states from applying them against married couples as well.

While the law establishes your rights as a married person, you can agree to change many of these rights by contractual agreement. This is called the premarital agreement (or prenuptial agreement). These contracts will be discussed in the next chapter.

3

PREMARITAL AGREEMENTS

As described in the last chapter, the marriage and property laws of your state govern your rights and obligations as a spouse. However, such laws are not necessarily written in granite. A man and a woman who are planning to marry can agree with each other to set aside the law as it would apply and create their own rules, most particularly with regard to the way property will be held during marriage and the way that matters will be handled in the event of a divorce. They do this by entering into a contract called a *premarital agreement* (also called *prenuptial agreement* or *antenuptial contract*). This chapter will describe the issues that are important to understand regarding premarital contracts. It will also touch upon other premarital transactions that can affect your rights and obligations.

THE PREMARITAL AGREEMENT

Say you have children from a previous marriage whom you want to be sure receive all of your property if you die. Or perhaps a rich person is marrying someone with less money and wants to make sure that the alimony rights of the soon-to-be spouse are restricted. The law as it applies to the rights of married persons might not serve your purpose.

A premarital agreement can short circuit the usual rules and make special ones to apply your marriage. A premarital agreement is a contract between people planning to marry that establishes the rights and responsibilities each spouse will have in the marriage, and what will happen should one spouse die or the marriage end in divorce. With a few exceptions, which will be discussed, a premarital agreement will be enforced by the courts regardless of how these matters would have been handled under the state's laws had no contract had been created.

The following questions are most frequently asked about premarital agreements:

Must the Contract Be In Writing?

If you are planning on entering a premarital agreement, be sure it is in writing. The reason for this is that a written agreement prevents misunderstandings about the terms and allows parties to fully comprehend the agreement they are making. Moreover, courts will usually not enforce an oral agreement. (In such cases, state law applies as if the contract was never created.)

There are rare exceptions to the rule that premarital agreements be in writing. The most notable exception involves a situation where one person believes that the nonwritten agreement is valid and performs according to the contract's terms. Under such circumstances, an oral agreement will be enforced if all of the following conditions exist:

- One party has kept the promises he or she made in an oral contract;
- That person performed believing the contract was valid and enforceable and relying on its provisions; and,
- As a result of keeping the oral promises, the performing party has suffered harm.

This is simply a matter of fairness. A person should not be allowed to reach an agreement, accept the other person's performance under the agreement and then wiggle out of their responsibility based on the technicality that the contract was not in writing.

Susan owned a house. She and Tom became engaged. They entered into an oral agreement which called for Susan to put Tom's name on her house once they were married. In return, Tom promised to put Susan's name on all of the stock he owned, giving her a one-half interest in all of his investments. The parties got married and pursuant to the agreement, Susan put Tom's name on her property. However, Tom refused to put Susan's name on his stock and sold the investments instead. Susan would be permitted to claim a one-half interest in the money if she could prove the terms of the oral agreement (which might be difficult if there were no witnesses) and that she acted to her detriment (i.e., she gave up ownership of half her house) in reliance on the agreement.

One night, after an evening of romance, Peter promised to leave Julie all of his property if he died after they were married. The two were married and Peter died without changing his will to provide for Julie as he had promised. Julie sued Peter's estate asking the court to award her all of Peter's property, using their oral agreement that once married, all of Peter's property would go to Julie if Peter died. Even though the court believed Peter had made the promise, the court ruled against Julie because the contract was not in writing and Julie's marrying Peter was not an act that was to her "detriment" since she was planning to do that anyway.

Does Money or Property Have to Be Exchanged for the Agreement to Be Upheld?

No, premarital agreements are an exception to the rule that something other than the promises must be exchanged for the agreement to be enforceable.

In order for a contract to be enforceable it must be supported by something lawyers call *consideration*. Consideration involves something of value given in exchange for the promises made, most often the payment of money in return for property or the performance of services. If there is no consideration, there is no contract, only empty promises that cannot be enforced by the law. Thus, if you hire a building contractor to remodel your house, your payment and the contractor's work are the consideration for the contract, which makes the terms of the agreement enforceable in court.

Some contracts permit mutual promises themselves to act as consideration, even though nothing of value is exchanged when the contract is entered. Premarital agreements are such contracts. The consideration which allows a premarital agreement to be enforced as a contract is the mutual promise of the parties to marry.

Does the Agreement Have to Be Fair?

Usually, but not always. Most states have laws that view premarital agreements as contracts entered into by people who are in a *fiduciary* relationship—that is, a relationship requiring both parties to act in utmost good faith and fair dealing toward each other. That puts an extra burden on the parties to treat each other correctly that does not exist in most other business contracts.

In order to make sure that a premarital agreement is proper, the court will usually require the existence of one of the following two conditions (and sometimes both):

Full Disclosure. Since the parties must deal with each other in good faith, each must fully disclose to the other, the extent, value and nature of their respective assets and property. Failure to do so might result in a court invalidating the agreement should a lawsuit ever be instituted to enforce its provisions.

Fair Provisions. To ensure that the agreement will be considered enforceable by the court, it should be fair to both parties. What is and what is not "fair" will be determined case-by-case. However, if one party does all the "giving" and the other all the "taking," there is a chance, although it might be a small one since courts prefer to hold people to their agreements, that the court would refuse to uphold the contract. (This is especially true if the unfair contract was agreed to by both parties without full disclosure of all pertinent facts.) Be very careful here. A contract is not "unfair" simply because you don't like it or because you got the worse end of the bargain.

If you and your fiancé want to enter into a premarital agreement, you should take the following steps:

- Both parties should have their own attorney represent them in the negotiations, or at least review the document to make sure that it is "fair." (Courts have often refused to enforce agreements when the aggrieved party was not represented by an attorney.) This is especially true when the party without the lawyer is the one whose rights are reduced to less than what they would be under state law.

In such cases, the person giving up rights should have the benefit of counsel, or the court may refuse to accept the agreement and apply state law.

- Both parties should give each other full disclosure of property, assets and obligations. Courts will often uphold a premarital agreement, *even if it is unfair*, so long as full disclosure was given. (Traditionally, it was the wife who was protected by the full disclosure provision. That sexist approach is waning as women achieve fuller equality in society.)
- The agreement should be fair. A fair agreement will often be upheld even if there was not full disclosure.

What Topics May a Premarital Agreement Cover?

Premarital agreements are most likely to be enforced when they deal with property rights. Here are examples of premarital agreements people often make regarding property rights.

Deciding What Happens to Property Upon the Death of One Party. The law, as mentioned in Chapter 2, establishes the rights of surviving spouses. However, parties can plan a different result through a premarital agreement. For example, if you have children from a previous marriage, you may desire a provision in a premarital contract that expresses your agreement with your fiancé that all property that you owned prior to marriage shall go to your children upon your death. Assuming that all other formalities have been properly followed in creating the premarital agreement and full disclosure was given, the court would most likely enforce the agreement.

How Property Is to Be Held During Marriage. Parties can agree ahead of time as to the specific way they will hold property. For example, in a community property state, a spouse's earnings can be deemed separate property. Or, separate property obtained during the marriage can be considered *marital property*. Marital property, like community property, is property that has been acquired by either party during the marriage, regardless of who holds title or whose earnings were used to obtain it.

Or, property that would be considered marital, may, by

agreement, be held separately. So long as the agreement is fair and full disclosure was given, the courts are likely to uphold the intent of the parties when they entered into the premarital agreement.

What Happens in the Event of Divorce?

At one time, courts were unlikely to enforce an agreement containing provisions to be followed in the event of a divorce because such agreements were considered to encourage marital break-up and were thus deemed to be against the public policy of supporting permanent, life-long marriages.

As society has changed and divorce has become more commonplace, if not the norm, the law has begun to change with it. A growing number of states (California, Colorado, Florida, Georgia, Illinois, Indiana, Maryland, Massachusetts, Missouri, Nebraska, New Jersey, Ohio, Oregon, West Virginia) now permit property provisions in a premarital agreement to specify what is to occur should the parties divorce. Issues of alimony may also be covered in some states, again with the provision that the agreement is fair and full disclosure was made.

The law is in a state of flux in this area. Some states permit property rights to be decided in the event of a divorce but not child support and alimony provisions. Other states allow both while some states still permit neither and states that have one set of rules today may change them tomorrow. The only way to know for sure is to go to the law library and look up the latest laws concerning premarital agreements as they apply in your state, ask an attorney, or attend a legal seminar at a law school.

When Will the Agreement Take Effect?

A premarital agreement becomes enforceable when the marriage ceremony is over. It is not enforceable before marriage.

Can the Agreement Be Done Away With?

If both parties agree in writing, premarital agreements can

be cancelled. The conduct of the parties may also invalidate an agreement. For example, in a Colorado case (a state that follows the law of community property), the husband and wife had agreed that they would not have any community property. Despite their agreement, after they were married, the couple treated their property at all times as if it were community, i.e., they took title to real estate in joint tenancy, pooled their bank accounts and otherwise treated their financial affairs as commingled. Upon their divorce, the court held that the parties, through their *conduct*, had abandoned the agreement.

If a premarital agreement becomes invalid, the laws of the state will apply to the rights and obligations of the parties.

Are There Tax Consequences in a Premarital Agreement?

A good rule of thumb in family law is that when property is exchanged, there are always potential tax consequences. When it comes to a premarital agreement, an exchange of property pursuant to the agreement will be subject to a federal gift tax if the value of the property transferred exceeds $10,000 (as of 1993).

What Subjects Cannot Be Dealt With in a Premarital Agreement?

There are areas of family life that the parties cannot decide ahead of time in a binding contract. These are:

The Amount of Support During Marriage. Agreements that regulate the amount of support to be paid by one spouse to support the other during marriage are generally considered invalid.

Who Gets Custody of Children. Agreements that establish which parent shall have custody of any children born in a marriage will not be recognized by a court. Decisions of this kind are made by courts based on the welfare of the child, not the agreement of the parties. (See Chapter 9.)

What the Amount of Child Support Will Be. Likewise, a court will not honor the provisions of a premarital agreement that seek to establish the amount of child support that will be paid.

How Marital and Family Relations Will Be Conducted. Courts are loathe to interfere in an ongoing marriage. For that reason, contracts that seek to regulate the couple's sexual relations, religious activities of the family or other such personal areas of life will not be enforced by a court.

Issues to Think About

If you want to prepare a premarital agreement, take the following steps:

- Each of you should provide full written disclosure. Each should exchange a list of all their respective property and debts.
- Identify what you want to accomplish. Perhaps you want to protect property from becoming a marital asset, or perhaps you are marrying someone who is in debt and you want to make sure your earnings are not used to pay them.
- Learn about the law in your state. You may not have to write up an agreement to accomplish what you want since it may already be the law.
- Hire at least one attorney. An attorney can only represent one person. If one of you will be giving up significant rights, he or she should have a lawyer—not only for advice but to ensure that the agreement will be upheld if it is ever challenged.
- Once the contract is written, read it carefully before signing. Make sure the agreement does what you wanted it to and make sure you understand each term. Don't allow yourself to be pressured. Once you sign, it will be presumed you knew what you were doing.

In summary, premarital agreements are best utilized to determine in advance what will happen to property upon a spouse's death or how property will be held and managed during the marriage. Thus, the mother who remarries may wish to reach an agreement with her fiancé that he will obtain no rights to her house by reason of the marriage so that it can be left to her children if she should die. However, provisions which seek to preestablish the rights of the parties upon divorce are more problematic in terms of enforcement, especially those agreements that involve the level of support to be paid, and agreements that involve the future raising of children are unlikely to be viewed with favor by courts. Thus, a premarital agreement that states the father will receive custody of the children of a marriage if the parties divorce would not be enforceable.

OTHER PREMARITAL TRANSACTIONS

There are other premarital transactions entered by parties in the expectation of marriage that the law is sometimes asked to deal with. The most notable are the following:

Breach of Promise to Marry

Lawsuits involving a breach of a promise to marry are rarely brought anymore, and the damages that can be awarded in such a suit are shrinking. At one time, a woman could sue for the loss of the prospective social status the marriage would have given her. Those were the days when marriage was considered a property transaction as well as a social contract. Today, such losses are not recoverable. Emotional damages sustained by a party as a result of the broken promise to marry may be allowed but such actions are increasingly considered anachronistic. However, any actual financial loss that results from the broken engagement, such as the cost for the purchase of a wedding gown or the loss of a deposit for a reception hall, can usually be recovered under the law.

Gifts Made in Contemplation of Marriage

Under most circumstances, once a gift is given and accepted, it is considered a legally completed transaction. As such, should the gift giver have a change of heart, he or she has no legal way to make the recipient return the gift.

However, gifts given in contemplation of marriage are different. They are considered to be conditioned upon the marriage actually taking place. If the marriage is called off, gifts such as engagement rings and other items given in contemplation of the marriage can be ordered returned. Likewise, third parties who give the engaged couple a wedding present, can demand a return of the gift should the marriage be called off.

As the culture moves in new directions, the field of family law struggles to follow. So far, we've discussed legal issues as they affect marriage and the intention to marry. In the next chapter we will address a new and unfolding area of the law: The manner in which it impacts upon people who choose to live together "without the benefit of clergy."

4

LIVING
TOGETHER

At one time in our history, if a man and a woman lived together in a sexual relationship without being married, it was considered immoral and improper conduct. That societal attitude found expression in the law, which called such relationships *meretricious* (involving unlawful sexual expression). Some states, such as Utah, Alabama and South Carolina, had laws making meretricious couplings a violation of the criminal law. All states viewed the parties involved in a meretricious relationship as bad, and undeserving of protection by the courts. (Common law marriages, however, were not viewed as meretricious.)

Then came the sexual revolution of the 1960s and 1970s. What was once considered immoral became commonplace. People who decided to "live together" without being married became a significant segment of society. Society had undergone a radical change and whenever society changes, slowly but surely, the law is bound to follow. Today, people who live together in a romantic relationship, whether heterosexual or homosexual, may have enforceable legal rights. When the relationship is all sweetness and light, that might not seem important. But when the parties break up they often begin to disagree about ownership of property and the right to money payments based on promises of support. This chapter will discuss the facts and circumstances that can give rise to such legal protection and will inform you of what you can do to protect yourself if you enter into such a "domestic partnership."

YOU MAY BE A CRIMINAL

While the law has been changing throughout the country, in some jurisdictions, the pace can be agonizingly slow. In many states, arcane laws remain on the books that permit authorities to punish "illicit" sexual activities. For example, Georgia has a criminal statute prohibiting sodomy (oral or anal copulation) between consenting adults. When this law was used to prosecute a homosexual, he brought it to the United States Supreme Court hoping that his rights to privacy would be upheld. Instead, on a 5-4 vote, the court sided with the state and the law was validated. Other states also have anti-sodomy laws on the books, including Rhode Island, Michigan, Minnesota, Nevada and Tennessee. (Texas and Kansas only prohibit sodomy between homosexuals.) States, such as New Jersey, New York and Florida, have had their anti-sodomy laws overturned by their courts.

Cohabiting, that is living together in a sexual relationship, may also be illegal (Arizona, Florida, Idaho, Massachusetts, Michigan, Mississippi, North Carolina, Virginia). These laws generally lie dormant. However, states will occasionally prosecute homosexual men, and the issue may be used in a child custody fight to deny custody to gay parents because they are engaging in felonious conduct.

LIVING TOGETHER CONTRACTS

One area where the laws have begun to change involves contracts entered between partners contemplating living together. Such contracts were once universally held to be unenforceable because such agreements were viewed as promoting immoral relationships. That began to change in California with a famous case known as *Marvin v. Marvin*. (NOTE: This is an evolving area of the law. How it will all play out and whether such contracts between homosexual couples will be enforced is still unknown.)

The second "Marvin" in *Marvin v. Marvin*, was the famous actor, the late Lee Marvin. The first Marvin was his former female partner, Michelle Triola Marvin. (She had changed her name to Marvin.) The two had lived together for seven years in a romantic and sexual relationship. After the relationship ended, Michelle sued Lee claiming that she had given up her career as a singer and acted as Lee's "companion, homemaker, housekeeper and cook." She had done this, she alleged, based on Lee's promise to share property he obtained during the relationship and to provide for her financial support for the rest of her life.

At first, the courts refused to hear the case at all because Michelle had lived with Lee knowing they were not married. That made the relationship meretricious and under the law, Michelle was simply out of luck. After the trial court dismissed her case, Michelle's lawyer took the case to the California Supreme Court, which issued a dramatic ruling that radically changed the law in California and began the ongoing trend in the country toward recognizing the rights of unmarried people who live together.

Specifically, the California Supreme Court made the following rulings:

- Contracts between unmarried partners would henceforth be enforceable unless the contract was a sex-for-hire-type arrangement. However, if there were other aspects fundamental to the relationship, such as those alleged by Michelle (homemaking, companionship and cooking, etc.), the law *would* be available to enforce the contract, even though the parties had sex outside of marriage as part of their relationship.

- The court didn't stop there: Not only would the court enforce formal contracts, it would enforce agreements "of partnership or joint venture" or other such contracts created by implication based on the *conduct* of the parties. In other words, the way people who live together act toward each other during their relationship could later be used to show the legal consequences the parties wished their relationship to create.

- Still the court wasn't done: It ruled that one partner could bring an action in *quantum meruit*, that is, an action to recover the value of services rendered by that person in the relationship, if it could be shown that the services were rendered "with the expectation of monetary reward."

Suddenly, in California at least, living together in a sexual relationship without being married could have significant legal consequences. The concept of meretricious relationships began to sink into disfavor. People who cohabit can negotiate with each other and enter into a valid written or oral contract concerning their rights and obligation that will be enforced by the courts. Moreover, conduct can give rise to legal rights. For example, if two partners opened a joint bank account, does this indicate that they intended to share income that both earned? The court might have to decide.

(Ironically, after winning the right to bring the lawsuit in the California Supreme Court, Michelle lost the case based on the evidence presented at the trial court level and in subsequent appeals on the trial court's decision. [Michelle was awarded $104,000 for "rehabilitation." Lee was able to have the Court of Appeals overturn that verdict, leaving Michelle with virtually nothing.] Thus, while her legal struggle did little to benefit her individually, the case of Marvin v. Marvin opened a door that much of the country is now in the process of entering. Also, Michelle's difficulties illustrate that the right to sue is one thing but winning may be something else again.)

All states do not follow the legal doctrine enunciated in Marvin v. Marvin. Illinois, for example, has refused to pick up the gauntlet, ruling in a 1979 case, that Marvin-type relationships gave rise to no legal rights. Because each state is likely to take a different approach to the question, you are well advised to learn what law applies in your state. To do so without cost, go to your local law library and look in the civil and penal codes. There are also legal encyclopedias that will summarize the law. ("Witkin" is the most notable.) You should also research court cases in your state.* You can also contact an attorney if you have any questions.

---

* See HALT's book, *Using the Law Library* for easy-to-understand legal research techniques.

PREPARING A LIVING TOGETHER AGREEMENT

With the law reflecting dramatic uncertainty and dynamic change in the area of "informal" relationships, it behooves anyone who is planning to live with a lover to be sure that their mutual intentions are as specifically demonstrated as possible. This section discusses what can be done if people who live together want to create legal rights and what they can do if they do not.

Steps to Take If You Want to Create Legal Rights

People who love each other and wish to create mutual rights without formally marrying, or who wish to create these rights because they cannot legally marry (for example, if they are a gay or lesbian couple), should make their desires known as specifically as possible. This means you will have to enter into an agreement. Keep in mind that absent a written, oral or implied agreement (where the court infers an agreement based on the conduct of the parties), there will be nothing for the court to enforce.

Here are some suggestions:

Write a Contract. If you want your relationship to be viewed as a partnership or joint venture, say so in a *written* contract. (Oral contracts are enforceable but they may be difficult to prove unless there are witnesses.)

A living together contract should be approached seriously and with as much forethought as any other contract you agree to participate in. Before drafting it, think ahead. Remember, you are trying to accomplish by agreement what hundreds of years of jurisprudence and statute writing already gives married couples, so be as specific and detailed in your contract as you can. Ask each other, "what if" questions: What if we buy a house? What if one of us has to move because of a job transfer? What if we break up? Come to an agreement on each what-if, and place the terms of your agreement into your contract. Here are some tips:

- *Avoid mentioning the sexual aspects of your relationship.* You do not want a court to be able to invalidate your wishes based on a theory that the contract is based on sexual services.

- *Be specific.* If you want your relationship to give rise to property rights and/or support obligations, say so. If you want to be able to inherit property should one of the partners die, agree in the contract that each must write a will pursuant to the terms of the contract. (People can enter into contracts to make a will in states that do not recognize the legality of living together contracts.)
- *Be comprehensive.* Think about the issues you wish to agree upon. For example, how are debts to be handled? What about property acquired before the relationship as well as that acquired after you begin to live together? Who pays for what monthly expenses? What about the support in the event one of you becomes ill or the relationship dissolves? Speaking of which, what will happen to your property if the relationship does terminate?
- *Do not rely solely on the contract.* Some states refuse to enforce them. And even if your state would, you should be sure to take other action that will set the agreement in concrete and which the courts will have to enforce. For example, you may want to take title to property in both names to ensure that both have ownership rights. For more information on living together contracts, see Appendix 4 (Bibliography). You can also retain an attorney to negotiate and draft your contract, if you would rather not do so yourself.

Hold Joint Title to Property. Agreeing that you shall own property jointly is one thing. Making sure your desires are followed may be something else entirely, depending on where you live.

To make sure your intentions to co-own property cannot be attacked by family members or others, or ignored by the courts, take title to property in both your names. For example, if you and your partner buy a house, make sure the title is held in joint tenancy or tenancy in common. (In a joint tenancy, if one partner dies, the other owns the entire property. This is known as "the right of survivorship." In a tenancy in common, the ownership interest of a deceased owner would be distributed pursuant to his or her will, or if there was no will, according to state law. For more details, see Chapter 2.) If you wish to remain the sole owner of property but wish to ensure that your partner receives your property upon your death, you can create a living trust.[*]

Automobiles, stocks and bonds, bank accounts, and any other type of property that is "owned" through a deed or certificate of title can also be put in both partners' names to embody the agreement or be made part of a living trust.

Commingle Your Assets. If you wish, you can take all of your assets and mingle them together. You can agree to have one bank account. You can put each other's names on vehicles or other property. You can give each other an interest in all of your property. Not only will this create an ownership right but it will be evidence of your desires in the event a court challenge is ever mounted against the living together contract or your rights as a couple.

Make Provisions in Life Insurance Policies and Employment Benefits. If you own a life insurance policy, you can name your partner as the beneficiary. You can request your employer to provide health, dental or other benefits for your partner, just as they do for a spouse. Most employers will not do so unless there is a formal marriage. But a few employers, most notably certain municipalities, have begun to recognize straight or gay cohabiting partners as being entitled to benefits such as health insurance, pension rights and etc. (At this time, there is no way to legally force your employer to recognize your arrangement as giving your partner the right to benefits.)

Write a Will. This is very important. So long as you are of sound and disposing mind and memory, you can legally dictate what will happen to your property and assets should you die. If it is in your will the courts will have to honor your desires, except in rare cases, such as if one of the living together partners has a spouse who is entitled to claim a share of the estate (see Chapter

---

[*] For a discussion of the different types of trusts available, see *How To Use Trusts To Avoid Probate & Taxes: A Guide to Living, Marital, Support, Charitable, and Insurance Trusts*, by Theresa Meehan Rudy, Kay Ostberg & Jean Dimeo in Association with HALT, Random House, 1992, $10.

2). That being so, you should provide for your partner in your will, leaving him or her the property that you desire and/or which you have agreed to leave upon your death in your living together agreement. Of special concern here: If you want to make sure your partner is in charge of the disposition of your property, name him or her as your executor (the person legally charged with settling the estate). Also, if you want your partner to take care of your children after your death, name him or her as their guardian, although that decision will ultimately be made by the courts in the best interests of the children.

Create a Power of Attorney. A *power of attorney* is a contract that permits another person to act on your behalf. It must be in writing. People generally use a power of attorney to allow someone else to handle one or more of their business transactions—paying bills, withdrawing money from a bank, selling or buying a house, even making investments. For example, you might authorize someone (called your *agent* or *attorney in fact*) to sell your car while on vacation. What does the power of attorney have with to do with cohabitation? Perhaps, a lot. A rather common tragedy that has befallen some partners has occurred when one of them became seriously ill or otherwise legally incapacitated. (Now, with many couples dealing with chronic or terminal illness, many partners are resorting to powers of attorney for health care and property management.) Should this happen, the ill partner's disapproving family could move in and legally exclude the lover from all aspects of the sick person's life.

The reason this can and does happen is this: Unlike married couples, cohabiting partners are not viewed by the law as a "family member" and each is considered a "stranger" to the other, regardless of the intimacy of the relationship. Thus, if one partner becomes incapacitated, the other partner is legally unable to give consent to doctors to provide health care and/or deal with issues of the ill person's financial affairs. However, a family member such as a parent or sibling can make these decisions—including the decision to exclude the well partner from all aspects of the incapacitated partner's life. This is true even if the partner and his or her family are estranged.

This is where powers of attorney come in. To ensure that each partner will remain vitally involved in the other's life should incapacitating illness or injury strike, two types of power of attorney can be prepared. These are called the *Durable Power of Attorney* and the *Durable Power of Attorney for Health Care.*

The word "durable" in durable power of attorney is the key here. A simple "power of attorney" becomes invalid upon the incapacitation of the person granting the power of attorney (called the *principal*). However a durable power of attorney remains in effect in the event of incapacitation and, in fact, can be designed to take effect *only* if the principal becomes incapacitated (commonly called a springing power of attorney).

The Durable Power of Attorney. A durable power of attorney gives the agent legal power to make financial and business decisions on behalf of the principal. The power can be unlimited or restricted in scope, depending on the wishes of the principal as set forth in writing in the durable power of attorney. For example, the power may permit the agent to conduct banking business but not sell property.

The Durable Power of Attorney for Health Care. This document, not available in all states, permits you to name the person you want to make your health care decisions should you ever be unable to make them yourself because of injury or illness. By giving your partner power of attorney for health care, you can prevent him or her from being excluded from your bedside should you become grievously ill or injured. (A durable power of attorney for health care can also direct whether or not you want life support systems to keep you alive if you fall into a coma or are terminally ill. This should be accompanied by a *living will* which can also make your wishes known in this regard.)

Powers of attorney must be filled out in the proper form and must usually be notarized or witnessed, depending on the state, to be effective. Also, they give enormous power over your affairs to the attorney in fact, so be sure he or she is completely trustworthy. Finally, they can be withdrawn at any time, so long as you are mentally competent to do so.

Let Your Family Know Your Desires. This isn't a matter of law but of common sense. If you want your partner considered a part of your family, if possible integrate your love relationship into your flesh-and-blood family. If they know and accept your circumstances, they are going to be much less likely to act in a way that would create difficulties and the need to resort "to the law."

Taking the steps outlined above are not without risks. For example, if you put your partner's name on your house, for better or worse, he or she becomes an owner of the house. If things fall apart, you could be forced to sell the house and give your former partner one half of its value. Likewise, if you place your partner's name on your bank accounts, there is nothing that can prevent him or her from absconding with the money. Thus, before you do anything that puts your estate or finances at risk, think of the sign at railway crossings: "Stop, look and listen:"

- Stop: meaning don't take action in the heat of passion.
- Look: meaning take your time. Before giving rights to your partner, be sure he or she is trustworthy and that the relationship is likely to be long-term. Also be sure that your partner doesn't have personal or financial difficulties that can ultimately hurt you. (For example, your partner's creditor might be able to attach your assets if you commingle your bank accounts.)
- Listen: meaning fully investigate your intended course of action before doing anything. Learn the state of the law where you live. Read about the pros and cons of the steps you are contemplating. Talk to others who have lived together to see if there is anything you can learn from their experiences.

In short, don't cross the tracks until you know you are not going to be hit by a train.

Steps to Take If You Do Not Want Legal Rights Created

Some people wish to live together but wish to ensure that no legal rights or obligations are created vis-a-vis their partner. If that is your desire, take the following steps:

Write a Contract. Just as a contract can create legal rights, it can make sure that such rights are not created. This agreement will be shorter and simpler than the living together agreement described above. You can simply state that:

- You and your partner are going to live together.
- You and your partner intend that all property that either of you may own at the time you move in together or which either of you might obtain in the future, shall be the sole and separate property of the person obtaining such property.
- That both of you give up any rights that may be created by the law as a consequence of living together.
- That neither of you has promised the other support or in any way to provide for the other in the event of illness, incapacity or the dissolution of the relationship.

You may also wish to set forth the responsibilities of each toward rent, utilities, food and other associated costs and expenses of living together. For example, the contract may provide that each is responsible for one-half of the rent and utilities, and that if one pays more than their share of such expenses, the other shall repay the money within 30 days.

Keep Your Affairs Separate and Apart. The Marvin case described above states that an agreement of partnership can be implied by the conduct of the parties. In order to prevent such an implication, make sure that you govern your affairs in a way that implies you do not want legal rights to be created. Treat every expense as if you were living alone. Do not commingle bank accounts. Do not pay for your partner's debts or other financial obligations (unless an agreement is signed stating that such payment does not constitute an agreement to pay such debts or create an implication that a living together partnership has been created). Each should pay one-half of the rent and utilities. In other words, keep your business and financial affairs separate and apart in every way.

This concludes the discussion of marriage and living together. As we have seen, if you and your partner marry or choose not to, the legal rights and obligations between you can be affected. However, there is an area of family law where this distinction is of much less importance. That is the topic of parenting children, which will the discussed in the next section.

PART 2

PARENTS & CHILDREN

5

BECOMING
A PARENT

The choice to have a child is probably the most important decision that anyone can make in their life, both personally and in relationship to society and the law. At one time the issue of having children was relatively cut and dried. It is a different story in the modern world. With new medical advances, the prevalence of divorce, the sexual revolution, and the political battles surrounding abortion, the subject of parenthood has become an intense emotional and legal battleground. This chapter will tackle the legal issues surrounding "becoming a parent," such as proving paternity and maternity, adoption, surrogate parenthood and birth control. (Chapter 9 will deal with issues of custody and visitation and Chapter 10 will cover the topic of child support.)

THE RIGHT TO NOT BECOME A PARENT

As hard as it may be to believe, it wasn't too many years ago that the state claimed a right to govern one of the most intimate areas of human life: the decision whether to have a child. Many states banned artificial birth control, even into the middle of the 20th century. Most states also made abortion a criminally prosecutable offense for both the doctor and the woman. In fact, it is only in relatively recent times that the courts have removed legal restrictions, based on the constitutional right to privacy.

The Right to Use Birth Control

By 1965, most state laws prohibiting or restricting the use of birth control devices had been repealed. Today, adult men and women, whether single or married, have the legal right to obtain contraception, albeit some methods such as "the pill" must be FDA-approved and prescribed by a doctor.

But what about minors? Can they obtain contraception without parental consent? The law is still unfolding in this area, but the answer appears to be yes. Laws that have sought to restrict the right of minors to obtain birth control without a parent's consent have generally been overturned by courts and many states specifically permit such access by minors. To learn the status of the law in your state, ask your doctor, your attorney, or look up the law in the law library.

The Right to Obtain an Abortion

Prior to the landmark case of *Roe v. Wade*, the states were free to determine the law of abortion as each saw fit. By 1973, some had begun to legalize the procedure. In most states, abortion remained illegal. Then the United States Supreme Court issued the Roe decision and the right to abortion became a constitutional right.

States are permitted by Roe to regulate abortion, but only under the following formula:

- In the first trimester of pregnancy, the state may not prohibit abortion.
- In the second trimester, the state may regulate abortion "in ways that are reasonably related to maternal health." This seems to permit limited state regulation during this period and indeed, some states have enacted laws restricting abortion (see below).
- In the last trimester the state may promote "its interest in the potentiality of human life" by regulating and denying

abortion except where necessary to preserve "the life or health of the mother."

The following summary is the current status of the law on abortion, an area of jurisprudence ever subject to change:

- *Roe v. Wade,* while somewhat modified, continues to be the law of the land.
- It is illegal for the federal government to finance abortions for poor women receiving Medicaid benefits (commonly known as "the Hyde Amendment").
- Family planning clinics that receive federal funds may discuss abortion, a prohibition on such talk having recently been repealed.
- While they may not prohibit the procedure, states may partially regulate the delivery of abortion services. For example, in Pennsylvania, a 24-hour waiting period has been allowed along with other restrictions such as mandatory education about the development of a fetus to all women seeking abortion.
- Minors cannot be prohibited from obtaining an abortion. However, they may be required to obtain the consent of a parent or, in the alternative, the consent of a court.
- The father of a fetus cannot prevent the mother from obtaining an abortion, whether the couple is married or unmarried.

Abortion is an issue that is not going to go away. If you want specific information about the status of the law in your state, contact a family planning organization, or look up the law in a local law library.

The Right to Give Up a Child for Adoption

A woman has the right to give her child up for adoption. (For a more complete discussion of adoption, see page 56.) A woman who gives up her child for adoption will be given a specific time frame within which she may be able to change her mind—most typically, six months, although in some states, the time limit is much shorter. For example, in Maryland, the birth mother has 30 days, or until the adoption decree becomes final, to change her mind, while in Florida, once the birth mother gives her consent, it's irrevocable.

The birth mother may also be able to have the expenses of her pregnancy paid for by the adoptive parents. However, she may not profit from placing her child up for adoption (she may not "sell" her baby). Also, once the adoption is complete, her identity will usually be hidden from the child. Her name will be taken off the birth certificate and other measures will be taken to protect the anonymity of both the birth parents and the adopting parents. One more point: The father of the child, if known, must also consent to the adoption or the father must be found by a court to have given up his parental rights. If the father refuses to consent and wishes an active involvement in the child's life, no adoption will be able to take place.

BECOMING A PARENT

There are several ways under the law to become a parent. They include:

- Being the biological parent of a child.
- Legally adopting another person.
- Surrogate parenthood.

("Foster parents" are not parents, being more akin to legal guardians.)

Establishing Biological Parenthood

The law has the right to establish who is the biological father of a child. This is usually done in court in a proceeding called a *paternity suit.* (Maternity is rarely an issue since the mother and child are always named on the birth certificate.) Paternity suits are usually brought in one of the following three circumstances:

- If the mother wants to prove a man is the father of her child so that she can obtain child support.
- If the state wishes to prove paternity so that it can seek reimbursement for welfare payments made to the mother.

- If a man seeks to prove he is the father of a child and is thus entitled to parental rights. (See Chapter 6.)

(A child can also seek to prove he or she is a child of a parent. Most frequently, this kind of case occurs in lawsuits involving a deceased person's estate.)

Evidence used in court to prove paternity can include whether the mother had sex with the man in question, whether the relations occurred at a time in the woman's cycle when she was likely to get pregnant and whether the man treated the child as his own such as by paying support, living with the child, acting as a father, or otherwise providing for the child's welfare.

Blood tests and DNA analysis are also useful, especially if they *disprove* paternity. Blood tests may or may not be admissible as evidence in court to prove parenthood. Of particular interest in this area is the newly developed *human lucecyte antigen* (HLA) test (involving white blood cells), a test that can not only disprove paternity with astonishing accuracy, but which can also establish, with a high level of probability, whether a man and a woman are the parents of a given child. As a result of this new scientific advance, many states now permit the HLA test to be admitted in court to prove parenthood (Arizona, California, Florida, Iowa, Idaho, Kansas, Massachusetts, Minnesota, New York, Ohio, Oklahoma). A few states continue to refuse HLA tests as proof of paternity (Georgia, Utah, Virginia, Wisconsin). Other states have yet to take an official position either in the statutes or court decisions on the issue.

In some cases, the law will assume that a man is the father of a child. This is known as a *legal presumption.* Most notably, this occurs if a child is conceived while the mother is married and living with her husband in the marital relationship. In such circumstances, the law will presume that the husband is the father of the child—in many states, whether or not that is biologically true. The purpose for this legal rule is to prevent husbands from denying paternity in the event of a divorce and to ensure that a man who has had a father/child relationship is not later able to sever that bond when a divorce is pending and he doesn't want to have to pay child support.

Proving paternity can be very important to the child and both parents. Once a man is found to be the father of a child, he is subject to all of the responsibilities and rights of parenthood.

For example, the court can order him to pay child support. Also, the child will have inheritance rights (unless written out of a will by the father). On the other hand, the father can use proof of paternity to obtain court orders for visitation or custody. (See Chapters 9.)

The Process of Adoption

People can also become parents of children by legal decree in a process known as adoption. This may be easier said than done, however. While there are between 1–2 million couples who want to adopt, there are only about 114,000 adoptions that go through each year.

An adoption is a legal proceeding brought in court which creates the same relationship under the law between the adopting parent(s) and adopted child as they would have were they biologically parent(s) and child. There are several kinds of adoption:

Agency Adoption. An adoption agency is a state-operated or regulated organization which acts as an intermediary between adopting and biological parents, and which investigates the adopting parents to determine whether they are suitable to assume the parental role and to ensure that the adoption will be in the best interests of the child. Agencies also take steps to protect the confidentiality of the adopting and biological parents and handle all of the paperwork.

Independent Adoption. Agency adoptions are frustrating for many who desperately want to become parents because agencies can take years to accomplish the paperwork and because in many parts of the country, it is difficult to adopt an infant through an agency (especially if the child is of a different race from the parents). As a result, many people who have the means to do so will adopt a child through a process known as the independent adoption.

In an independent adoption, the adopting parents contract with the mother of an unborn child to adopt her child. Frequently, the adopting parent(s) will pay for the biological mother's medical expenses in bearing the child and may provide her with other forms of support during her pregnancy. When the baby is born, the adopting parents take the child home from the hospital and then file a petition for adoption in court. The court will order a home study conducted by the social welfare department. The biological mother and father will have to give their written consent—or a court order will have to be obtained doing away with this requirement. (A parent who has abandoned the child or has been found guilty of repeated abuse may have their parental rights stripped, after which their consent will not be required.) Once all of the work has been done, then the court will issue the order granting the adoption if it is in the best interests of the child. If the adoptive parents are not deemed capable of raising the child or of providing a proper home, the adoption will be denied. If the adopting parents are deemed capable, the child's birth certificate will be ordered changed, with the adopting parents listed in the revised document as the mother and father of the child. (Not all states permit this form of adoption.)

There are ministers and lawyers who arrange independent adoptions, as well as those who can help adopting parents find a child in a foreign country who may be available for independent adoption. To obtain more information on adoptions, see Appendix 5.

Step-Parent Adoptions

A step-parent adoption is a form of independent adoption, usually involving one biological parent and his or her spouse, who seeks to become the legal parent of the family's children. In order for a step-parent to adopt the child of his or her spouse, the other biological parent will have to consent, be dead, or be found to have given up all parental rights—usually through *abandonment*, or child abuse. (Abandonment is usually defined as the failure to support or have meaningful contact with the child for 12 months.) A home study will be conducted which will look at the interaction between the child and adopting parent, the home life of the couple and other issues concerning the child's welfare. Then, if all consents are obtained and if the home study recommends the adoption, the court will issue the adoption decree. Once the order is entered, the step-parent is deemed by the law as the legal parent of the child with all of the rights and responsibilities involving that important relationship.

Jane and John were divorced. They had one child, named Edward. For two years, John refused to pay child support for Edward, and other than sending him a Christmas card each year, he refused to have anything to do with his son. Jane later married Harold. Harold and Edward got along very well and the family decided that Harold should adopt Edward and become his legal father. Accordingly, they filed a petition for adoption in court.

When John was served with the adoption papers, he was furious. Edward was his son and he was not about to give up his parental rights. He hired a lawyer and contested the adoption. The court ruled against John and in favor of Harold, stating that John's refusal to support the child or have any meaningful relationship with him constituted legal abandonment. Edward wanted the adoption too, and since he was 12, the court was willing to listen to the boy's desires. (It is up to the court to determine the welfare of the child, not the child. However, if a child actively resisted the adoption, the court would take those feelings into account.) The court found that it was in Edward's best interest for the adoption to go through and thus ordered the adoption even though John refused to consent.

Before undertaking an independent or step-parent adoption, be as sure as you can that the matter will go smoothly. That is, try and "get your ducks lined up in a row" before beginning the process, if that is possible. This is especially important in light of the fact that independent and step-parent adoptions can be and often are, contested, and absent abandonment, neglect or child abuse, if one parent refuses to consent, the adoption cannot go through.

Biological parents who give up their child for adoption can also change their minds for a period of time, usually six months. This can have emotionally devastating consequences. For example, in a recent case, a single woman became pregnant, and believing she could not adequately care for her child, agreed to give up her baby for adoption. When the biological father learned he had a child, he refused to consent to the adoption and married the mother. She then changed her mind about the adoption because she felt she was now in a position to adequately raise her baby. (This all occurred within several weeks of the birth.) For two years the biological and adopting parents fought it out in court over which family should be allowed to raise the child as their own. After two years, the child was finally ordered returned to the biological parents, despite the fact the little girl had lived with the adopting parents her entire life and considered them her parents. The reason? The parents had legally refused to consent to the adoption and thus, the adoption had never gone through.

Adult Adoptions

Adopting a child can be difficult because of the state's interest in protecting the welfare of minors. Adults, on the other hand, do not require such protection. Thus, so long as all of the parties consent to an adult adoption, the court will usually grant the request. There are relatively few adult adoptions, although some homosexual couples are beginning to use this device to create a legal relationship where the law would otherwise deny it.

Qualifications to Become an Adoptive Parent

The courts look at the life circumstances of people who wish to adopt to determine whether they are "appropriate." Here are some of the issues courts look to:

A Single Parent vs. a Couple. Many states remain reluctant to allow single people to adopt and some also require couples to be married. Other states permit single and unmarried people to adopt.

Age. To adopt, you have to be an adult. Some states require that you be at least ten years older than the child. Since any adoption has to be in the best interest of the child, elderly people who are unlikely to be able to fulfill their parental role may have difficulty adopting a young child. (Agencies may refuse to allow older people to adopt.)

Race. Many states are reluctant to sanction interrace adoptions although their rationale will be couched in other than racial terms so as to avoid civil rights problems. Only two states prohibit using race as a criteria when determining the suitability of adoption (Connecticut, Kentucky).

Religion. Religion, like race, raises emotional issues. Some states require, when practicable, that a child be placed with adopting parents of the same religion as the birth parents. Two states (Connecticut, Kentucky) prohibit such considerations. Religion, like age, and race, will probably be considered in determining the best interests of the child.

Homosexuality. At one time it was presumed that it would be inappropriate to place a child by adoption into a gay or lesbian household. That is beginning to change. Today, gays and lesbians, either individually or as couples, are beginning to be allowed to adopt children. So far, most of the cases are in California or New York. Expect the law to come to grips with the issue of whether homosexuals should be allowed to adopt children in the very near future, with courts basing their decisions on "the best interests of the child."

Surrogate Parenthood and Artificial Insemination

With the many advances of medical science in the area of fertility and child bearing, new medical procedures are now available that not only have medical consequences but also have a significant legal impact. The most important of these are surrogate parenthood and artificial insemination.

Surrogate Parenthood. In a surrogate parenthood, a woman allows herself to be artificially inseminated with the sperm of a man whose mate is unable to conceive. After she gives birth, the biological father and his spouse take the baby home and raise it as their own. Thereafter, the surrogate mother gives up all parental rights and obligations and has nothing further to do with the child.

That is the theory. But when it comes to matters of the heart, things never go as smoothly in real in life as they do in theory. Some surrogate mothers find that they do not want to give up their child. This has led to bitter lawsuits and custody fights.

In order to overcome such possible conflicts, surrogate contracts have been created whereby the birth mother agrees in writing to release the child to the family who has arranged for the surrogate pregnancy. Some of these contracts also call for the birth mother to be paid for her "services." This type of arrangement may run afoul of laws that prohibit selling babies. Also, some lawyers claim that a surrogate birth is akin to an independent adoption and thus, the birth mother should be given time within which she can change her mind before giving up all parental rights. Courts in several states have struggled with the issue.

As of this writing, there are no state statutes dealing with the issue. Thus, each state court must grapple with the issue and fashion rules and decisions regarding the legalities of surrogate parenthood and surrogate contracts. To date, there are few decisions in this area. To find out whether your state has any specific policies about surrogate parenthood, look up the issue in your law library.

Artificial Insemination. Artificial insemination (sometimes known as alternative insemination) is much less controversial. (Artificial insemination can be defined as a conception which is created without sexual intercourse between the biological parents.) This process allows a woman to be impregnated with a man's sperm. Often this is done through a medical procedure although many women have been able to artificially inseminate themselves. The sperm donor is usually anonymous, meaning that there are no parental rights for the biological father to worry about. This is also true if the woman is married. In such cases, the woman's husband is deemed the legal father of the child, regardless of biology. However, if the woman is unmarried and the sperm donor is known, he may incur support and other legal obligations of fatherhood and may be entitled to the rights (visitation, custody, etc.). The rules in each state will vary, so if you intend to be a donor or to become inseminated, be sure that you know all of the possible legal ramifications.

This closes our discussion of becoming a parent and the law. As with many issues of family law which involve the most intimate of human behavior and decisions, the law is ever unfolding, ever in a state of change—and may dramatically vary in different parts of the country. However, once parenthood has been established, the rights and obligations of parents and children are less controversial. We now turn to these issues as we discuss the rights and obligations of parenthood.

6

BEING
A PARENT

Society has long recognized the importance of child rearing, which is reflected in the laws that govern "parenting." Some of these laws will be found in state statutes. Court decisions also impact the area, with courts being increasingly asked to involve themselves in the rearing of children. As a result, there is a lot of law to be found that governs this vital family relationship.

This chapter will explore the questions most parents have about their legal rights and obligations, such as: What are your rights as a parent to control the upbringing of your children? When can you be held responsible for the wrongful acts of your children? When and under what circumstances do the obligations of parents toward their children end? We will start the discussion with an overview of your obligation to support your children.

PARENTS' OBLIGATION TO SUPPORT THEIR CHILDREN

Your first and foremost legal obligation toward your children is the obligation of support. But what does that mean? And under what circumstances can you receive the state's help in supporting your children if you do not have the means to provide such support?

What Is the Meaning of "Support"?

Many people think of the term "child support" as referring to the money a divorced parent pays to a former spouse who has been awarded custody of the couple's children. (See Chapter 10.) But the concept of child support is broader and deeper than that. *Both* parents have the legal obligation to support their children, whether the parents are married, single or divorced, and whether their children live with them or not. (At one time, the support obligation was solely the father's, but that has changed.)

The amount and extent of support a parent owes his or her child depends on two factors: Ability to pay and the extent of the child's needs. That being said, the following principles should be kept in mind:

You Must Provide Your Children With the Necessities of Life. Just as spouses are responsible for the expenses of each other's "necessities," so too are parents responsible for such needs of their children. Thus, you must adequately feed and clothe your children, make sure they receive necessary medical care, provide shelter, make sure their home environment is clean and wholesome, and the like. (For a more detailed discussion of the legal concept of necessities, see Chapter 2.)

If You Fail to Meet this Obligation, You May Face Court Action. If you refuse or are unable to provide for your child, you can face severe court action. For example, civil authorities can remove your children from your home if the refusal to provide support is so bad that it constitutes abuse or neglect. If the child is removed, a court proceeding will be brought in the juvenile court, which will decide whether to return the children to your care, place them in a foster home or place them with a relative.

You may also face criminal prosecution if your failure to provide for your children constitutes abuse or neglect. Willful failure to support a child is usually a *misdemeanor* (punishable by a fine and a year or less in jail). However, if the neglect or abuse injures or kills the child, the parent can be prosecuted for a *felony* and spend years in state prison. A parent who willfully fails to pay court-ordered child support can also be put in jail for contempt of court.

You Can Also Be Sued. This usually happens in family court, when the custodial parent seeks back child support that has been ordered by a court. In some cases, your child, or someone acting on his or her behalf, can bring a civil lawsuit against a parent who refuses to provide support for necessities. A successful suit will result in a court order requiring the parent to pay a specific amount of money for the child's support, similar to the familiar child support order made in divorce decrees.

How Long Does the Child Support Obligation Last?

The duration of a parent's child support obligation is not indefinite but will end upon the following event:

When Your Child Reaches Majority. Generally, you are not required to support a child who has legally become an adult (reached majority) at age 18. However, in a divorce situation, some courts have ordered a parent to pay for higher education as an incident of child support, usually because the parents agree to extending the support in a marital settlement agreement.

When Your Child Becomes Emancipated. You may also be relieved of your support obligation if your child becomes *emancipated*. When a minor becomes legally emancipated, the "child" assumes responsibility for his or her own life as if an adult. That means that you are no longer required to provide support, just as if the child were a legal adult.

Whether or not a child is emancipated depends on the facts of each situation. (The issue most often comes up when a parent seeks to terminate a child support order after a divorce, based on the child's emancipation. However, sometimes parents seek a court order when they can no longer control their child.) The following factors tend to prove emancipation:

- Enlistment in the military
- Marriage
- Providing for self-support
- The child moving from home and leading a life independent of parental authority and control

If the child still lives at home, or remains dependent on you for food, money, clothes and other necessities, emancipation will not exist.

If the circumstances that led to emancipation change, the emancipation may revert and you would again be responsible for support. For example, if a child moved away from home at age 16 and lived independently of parental control and support, he or she could become emancipated. However, that child would again be deemed a minor if he or she moved back home and submitted to your parental authority before reaching age 18.

If Your Child Dies. The obligation of a parent to support a child ceases at death.

Is There Any Way to Support My Children If I Die?

The primary method most parents use to protect their children in the event of death is life insurance (life insurance policies are discussed in Chapter 13) or in the way a deceased parent's estate is distributed pursuant to a will or the law of the state. Many better-off individuals also choose to create a trust for their children to provide support upon death or even during the child's adult life.

The government has created a Social Security benefit to help provide for the surviving children of deceased workers. This is called the Survivors Program.

To be considered a survivor for Social Security purposes, at least two things must happen:

- The deceased person must have qualified for the program by working for a minimum period of time and paying Social Security taxes based on his or her earnings; and
- The young person must legally be considered a child of the deceased worker.

Payments under the Social Security Survivor's Program can amount to hundreds of dollars per month, depending on the earnings of the deceased worker and how long he or she worked before dying. Children must be under age 18 to qualify (or become disabled before age 22). For more information on the Survivor's Program, contact your local Social Security office.

What If I Can't Provide for My Child?

Some parents are so poor that they cannot adequately provide for their children. In such cases, the state has programs to help, known in the vernacular as "welfare." If you are poor, there are several welfare programs that are available to assist you to provide for your children:

Aid to Families with Dependent Children (AFDC). The most well-known welfare program is AFDC. AFDC is financed primarily by the federal government and is administered by each state. To qualify for AFDC, you will have to pass a "means test." That means your family's income and the value of your property must be below a cut-off point set by your state's laws. The benefit is based on the number of children you have. Some states will pay a few hundred dollars a month and some will pay as much as $800 or more.

There has been much litigation over the attempts by states to limit AFDC payments and over issues of state intrusion into the lives of recipients. From among these many lawsuits, have come the following rulings:

- A state cannot require long waiting periods for people moving from other locations before they are entitled to AFDC.
- A state can require a home inspection of the homes of AFDC recipients to make sure that fraud isn't being committed.
- Non-custodial parents can be required to reimburse the government for welfare payments made to support his or her children. In such cases, child support owed the custodial parent must be paid to the state rather than the parent.
- AFDC recipients must report all income and gift money they receive to the welfare department. Depending on the rules, the level of AFDC may be reduced if the income or value of the gift exceeded an amount established in each state's laws.

> Alice and Al were divorced. Al was ordered to pay Alice $200 per month in child support. Instead, he left the state and no payments were made. Alice lost her job and applied for AFDC to help support her children. She received $500 per month.
>
> Later, Al got a good job and paid Alice all of his back child support. Alice had to report the income to the welfare office and her benefits were reduced. Thereafter, the state brought an action against Al requiring him to pay the state the child support rather than Alice, so long as she was receiving AFDC benefits.

Rules and requirements governing AFDC can be expected to change dramatically in the years to come. (For example, it is likely that welfare recipients may have to work or obtain training to qualify for long-term benefits, and there is a federal proposal to limit welfare to a period of two years.) For more information and for details of the manner in which the program operates in your state, contact your state social services department or organizations that assist the poor, such as legal aid offices.

Medicaid

Medicaid is a government financed health insurance program designed to provide health care for people with no ability to pay, including children. In order to qualify for Medicaid, a family must be in poverty, based on income and property. (The rules of eligibility can vary dramatically from state to state. Generally, an applicant can't have assets in excess of the $1,500 to $3,000 range.) Unlike AFDC and other forms of welfare, the working poor can often qualify for Medicaid.

Each state offers different levels of Medicaid benefits. However, since the program is partially funded by the federal government, it requires that each state cover the following minimum medical benefits:

- Hospitalization
- Outpatient services
- Physicians' services
- Lab tests and X-rays
- Nursing home care
- Transportation services

States are free to add additional benefits if they choose to do so. Some add dental care, speech therapy, prescribed drugs, eye glasses and preventive health benefits such as child immunizations.

If you are interested in applying for Medicaid, contact your state's welfare department, health department or Social Security office.

Food Stamps

Another valuable program to help people provide for their children is food stamps. Food stamps are vouchers that can be used like money to buy food, such as meat, vegetables and milk. (They cannot be used for items such as cigarettes and liquor.) The eligibility levels to receive food stamps will vary from state to state. People who are eligible for AFDC are eligible for food stamps. However, even if you are not eligible for AFDC (for example, if your earnings are too high to be eligible) you may nevertheless be eligible to receive food stamps. So, if you have a low income, contact your local welfare department to learn the rules of food stamp eligibility.

THE RIGHT OF PARENTAL CONTROL

Parents have substantial legal control over the lives of their children. The scope of this right is not indefinite. For example, a parent cannot abuse or neglect a child. (See Chapter 11.) Still, parents have the substantial right to make most decisions about the upbringing of their children without state interference.

Education

You, as a parent, are free to choose the type of education your children receive. For example, the state cannot compel your child to attend public school if you wish to send your children to private or parochial school. However, the state may not pay for parochial school services that would be paid if the child attended public school. This may be changing though. The U.S. Supreme

Court recently permitted a deaf child's sign language interpreter to be paid from public funds even though the child was attending parochial school. Likewise, you can provide home schooling for your children if you can show you are providing a minimum level of education. Parents do not have the right to withhold education from their children.

If you don't want your children to be exposed to certain ideas and concepts, you may or may not have power to prevent it, depending on the issue involved. For example, you do not have the right to control public classroom curriculum, although you can certainly participate in the political process that influences the setting of your state's curriculum requirements. (The political involvement of parents has caused many school districts to limit the information provided in sex education classes or make a child's attendance for these classes subject to parental consent.)

There is a limit to the power of parents to influence laws that govern education. For example, a state cannot authorize public school authorities to lead prayer in the schools, no matter what the electorate wants, nor can a state require that "creationism" be taught as science.

Health Care

You have the right to make health care decisions on behalf of your minor children and must give your consent to most medical treatment your child receives, except in an emergency. However, this right is not absolute. For example, you cannot refuse necessary medical care because of your religious beliefs. (When Jehovah's Witness parents have refused to consent to a needed blood transfusion because it was against their religion, juvenile courts have been awarded custody of the children so that they could give the required consent. Similarly, Christian Scientist parents have been criminally prosecuted for relying on prayer rather than medical care to assist their seriously ill children who have died when they did not receive timely medical care.) Also, children can now obtain drug or alcoholism rehabilitation, birth control and in some cases, abortions, without parental consent.

Religious Upbringing

You also have the right to determine the religious upbringing of your children, or the lack thereof. This is not a problem when parents agree. But when they don't, especially in a divorce context, it can prove a thorny issue.

Contracts

Children do not have the legal right to enter into contracts, and any contract a child enters can be voided by his or her parents. Thus, if a 16-year-old agrees to buy a car, his or her parents can prevent the purchase.

(There are other incidents of control over minors, such as the choice of residence and the manner of discipline, that only become issues in cases of divorce, emancipation or juvenile court proceedings. These and other issues will be discussed in Chapters 9 and 10.)

PARENTAL RESPONSIBILITY FOR ACTS OF THEIR CHILDREN

If a child commits an act that give rise to a civil liability (the child does something for which he or she can be sued), the parent can be held liable for the damages. For example, if your child throws a baseball through a window, you can be compelled to pay for the cost of repair. This is permitted because most states have passed laws known as *vicarious liability statutes*. To prevent parents from facing potential financial ruin, vicarious liability statutes usually place a limit on the amount of money a parent can be forced to pay for the civil wrongs of their minor children, generally about $15,000.

Under certain circumstances, parents can be sued for the full amount of damages caused by the civil wrongs of their child. Thus, if a person who was damaged by a child's misbehavior could prove that the parents were negligent in the manner in which they supervised their child and that the poor supervision allowed the child to cause the damage, then the parents can be sued for the full amount of the damage—based on their own negligence.

Young Billy was a troubled child who was known in the neighborhood as a boy who could not be trusted. One day, Billy decided to throw rocks from his mother's rock garden over the fence at a neighbor's house. One rock hit the neighbor in the head, knocking him unconscious and causing him serious injury. The neighbor's medical and legal damages were $25,000.

The neighbor sued Billy and his parents. The parents tried to limit their liability to $10,000, the amount permitted by their state's vicarious liability law. However, the neighbor also sued Billy's parents for negligently failing to control Billy's behavior. At the trial, neighbors testified that Billy was often in trouble and had once been arrested for throwing rocks. The jury found Billy liable for the rock throwing and the parents liable for negligent supervision of Billy. Thus, the parents had to pay the entire $25,000.

Generally, parents are not criminally culpable for the crimes of their children. However, this might be changing. For example, in Los Angeles, parents have been arrested for permitting their children to join gangs. In many parts of the country, parents have been arrested after their child has shot someone with the parents' gun, because the parents kept their weapon where children were reasonably likely to be able to get at it.

Issues of child support and parental control are rarely an issue that affect well-functioning families, as these decisions are personal and made informally within the family unit. However, when a family is dysfunctional and in discord, these issues often become hotly contested in the courts—either in divorce court or juvenile court.

The next part of this book deals with these unpleasant and emotional issues. First, we begin with a discussion of divorce, separation, annulment and death of a spouse. After that, we tackle the issue of property division, alimony and working with attorneys. We then move to the issue of establishing and enforcing child custody and support orders. And finally, in Chapter 11, we tackle the growing problem of family violence.

PART 3

WHEN A MARRIAGE ENDS

7

DIVORCE, ANNULMENT, SEPARATION & DEATH

All good things must come to an end—and that includes every marriage. The death of a spouse is the reason most marriages end, since the death of a spouse automatically terminates a marriage. The law also permits marriage to be terminated by court order, either through the process of *divorce* (sometimes called a *dissolution*) or by way of annulment. A court order of *legal separation* permits a couple to formally sever much of their marriage relationship, divide property and establish support levels and custody rights, just as in a divorce, while maintaining the legal status of husband and wife.

This chapter will focus primarily on divorce. It will address the legal grounds for the action, how "fault" divorces differ from "no-fault" divorces, and the nature of a contested divorce proceeding. The use of alternative dispute resolution (ADR) programs will also be discussed, as will issues that can arise because of an annulment, legal separation or death of a spouse.

DIVORCE

For better or worse, divorce has become a part of "the American way of life." The statistics are enough to give anyone pause: About 1.2 million divorces occur each year. Fully two-thirds of people who were recently married can expect to terminate their marriage through divorce. Having one spouse for a lifetime is growing increasingly rare.

These statistics, of course, do not tell the full story. Divorce is a family tragedy. The feelings of rejection, betrayal and failure can sometimes be overwhelming. Children are often hit hardest of all, torn apart emotionally as their once seemingly-secure family disintegrates before their eyes. Having to deal with the dispassionate realities of "the law," lawyers, judges and "going to court" often leaves divorcing spouses with the feeling that the process seems cruel and unjust.

Still, the system is what the system is. That being so, it is important for everyone contemplating or going through a divorce to know what lies ahead. Here is an overview of the process of divorce. The rules of law concerning property division, alimony, attorneys' fees and other issues will be covered in the next chapter.

Will I Need a Lawyer?

That depends on the complexity of your case and whether you and your spouse can negotiate a peaceful settlement rather than wage emotional and divisive combat in divorce court. If both spouses approach divorce with the attitude that they will do what is right and fair for *both* parties and the children, many divorces can be handled without a lawyer. In fact, self-help and do-it-yourself divorce materials abound for couples who can agree on how to end their marriage. However, if there is a lot of money at stake, a substantial disagreement on what property should be divided or a fight over custody, chances are one or more lawyers will have to be called in.

What Are the Grounds for Divorce?

Divorces used to be difficult to obtain. If you wanted a divorce, you used to have to prove that you were entitled to it based on the bad conduct of your spouse. That is far less true today. All states now permit some form of *no-fault divorce*, either as the sole grounds for terminating a marriage or in addition to traditional grounds (see below).

No-Fault Divorce. Several studies published in the 1960s indicated that having to prove "fault" did not save marriages but rather, made their termination more bitter and acrimonious. Thus was born the *no-fault divorce* reform movement.

Since the early 1970s, the no-fault movement has changed the face of divorce in most states. Gone is the need to air the dirty family laundry in order to present facts proving fault. Today, in no-fault states, spouses can obtain a divorce merely by alleging that the marriage suffers from "irreconcilable differences" or an "irremediable breakdown of the marriage." The testimony that the marriage has broken down with no hope of repair is sufficient in and of itself. No facts are even admitted into evidence to prove that the statement is true. Unlike the fault system, if one spouse does not want the divorce he or she will be unable to stop it.

Some states still do not permit this type of no-fault divorce but have other no-fault plans in place. The grounds requirement for a no-fault divorce might be *living separate and apart* from your spouse for a specified period of time. (This is available in about half of the states.) For example, in Alabama, the time required is 2 years. In Minnesota, the time is 180 days.

Another no-fault grounds for divorce is by *mutual consent decree.* If both parties agree, the court will award the divorce. Others are *incompatibility,* similar in concept to irreconcilable differences, and the existence of a previous court-ordered judicial separation.

Traditional Grounds for Divorce. Some states limit no-fault divorce so much that many people still must prove that there are grounds for a divorce. If you live in one of these states, such as New York or New Jersey, you may have to present facts about what went wrong with your marriage in order to get the divorce. That can be embarrassing or unpleasant.

The traditional grounds for "fault" divorce are as follows:

*   *Adultery:* Adultery is engaging in voluntary sexual intercourse with someone other than the adulterer's spouse.

- *Desertion:* Desertion (also called "abandonment") involves the willful absenting of one spouse from the household of the other.
- *Cruelty:* Cruelty refers to one spouse physically harming the other in all states that allow this ground for divorce. Some states have expanded the term to include non-physical suffering as well, sometimes known as "mental cruelty."
- *Incompatibility:* This refers to conflicts so deep in the relationship that the marriage can no longer be sustained.

If a divorce is requested based on fault, the defendant can attempt to prevent the divorce by proving that he or she did not engage in improper behavior. If that is shown, the divorce will not be granted. Another way to prevent the divorce is to show that there was an excuse for the acts committed. Defenses to divorce are rarely heard anymore because the spouse "at fault" is rarely "punished" anymore. (At one time, courts might award more property or alimony to the "wronged" spouse. But that is seldom true now.)

What Happens If We Agree to the Terms of Our Divorce in Advance?

Many divorcing couples don't fight at all, but agree in advance to the terms. In such cases, a *marital settlement agreement* will be completed by the couple and signed. It will then become the basis of the divorce *decree* (the final decision of the court).

In uncontested cases, one of the spouses will then file for the divorce. The other will be served with divorce papers. His or her *default* will later be taken and a divorce will be obtained pursuant to the terms of the marital settlement agreement. (A default occurs when the answer is not filed in a timely manner.) At the hearing for the divorce, the marital settlement agreement will be introduced into evidence. Its terms will provide the terms for the divorce degree which will also be brought to court for the judge to review and sign.

If the marriage is very short, the parties have no children and there is no property to be divided, some states permit a "summary divorce." A summary divorce is a simplified divorce procedure that can often be completed by mail. For details, contact the court clerk of your domestic or family court.

ALTERNATIVE DISPUTE RESOLUTION

ADR programs can be very beneficial to people who are divorcing, as well as to those who have long been divorced but who find themselves in a dispute in their post-divorce relationship. Not only can it save money, but it promotes positive dispute resolution rather than conflict. That being so, it is well worth investigating by any couple facing divorce, a child custody fight, a visitation dispute or other interpersonal conflict.

ADR is a concept of relatively recent vintage that can help you resolve your case so you can have an uncontested divorce. ADR is particularly useful in situations involving children, since it is in the interests of the children that their parents "get along" even if they will no longer live together as husband and wife.

ADR attempts to change disputes from "win-lose" to "win-win." The primary vehicle of ADR in divorce cases is *mediation.* Mediation occurs when when a neutral third party, who has training in dispute resolution, sits down with you and your spouse and helps you resolve the issues that are causing conflict in a spirit of fairness and mutual compromise.

Mediation offers many advantages:

- Studies show that families that mediate their differences have a substantially better after-divorce relationship than families that litigate their differences.
- Mediators use a variety of negotiating techniques to help spouses reach a mutually agreeable solution to their differences. The final decisions are the spouses', not the mediator's, because both have had a say in how to deal with the issues that are important to them.
- Mediation is far less expensive. It can save a divorcing couple a lot of money. As you will see from the brief description of contested divorces below, adversarial trials get very expensive, what with the cost of attorneys, expert witnesses and time taken away from more positive pursuits. If you can successfully resolve all of the issues in your case, ranging from property division to support to custody, you will be many dollars ahead.

- In some courts, mediation is free. Hourly rates for services that charge are often based on a sliding scale, ranging from $40 to $150. By comparison, fees for divorce lawyers range from $100 per hour to more than $200 per hour *for each spouse,* depending on the section of the country in which you live.
- Mediation is faster. In a traditional court setting, trials can stretch for many months or even into years.
- Mediation is confidential. The emotional and perhaps embarrassing issues that are raised in divorce and child custody difficulties will be kept private, as opposed to a trial where all of the proceedings are part of the public record. This is especially important when the mediation concerns children. The adversarial nature of a divorce trial can severely strain the ability of parents to communicate with each other and their children. Dealing with custody, visitation and child support in ADR can often short-circuit much of the bitterness and support positive family interaction. That can really help the children, who usually want to maintain a close bond with both their mother and father.

You can consult a lawyer for legal advice at any time during the process. If you wait until you've reached an agreement, try to find a lawyer who is open to mediation, who recognizes that your agreement reflects a mutual decision, and who will not give legal advice designed to refuel the fires that you worked so hard to extinguish.

There are several sources of mediation available:

The Court

Most divorce courts have mediation services available to couples at low or no cost. Much of the emphasis in the courts concerns settling issues involving children, with family counselors providing the mediation services. (This is often called *conciliation court.*) But there may also be marriage counseling available, as well as volunteer attorney mediators to help resolve property and support disputes.

Professional Mediation Services

There are professional mediators who earn their living by providing divorcing couples mediation services on all issues. These professionals can be invaluable in helping couples resolve property and support issues, and will also assist with custody and visitation disputes. Divorce attorneys and family counselors can often refer families to professional family law mediators. Mediation services should be listed in your Yellow Pages. Psychologists, family counselors and social workers may also offer such services. Many family counseling clinics will provide mediation and counseling and charge based on income.

Neighborhood ADR Centers

Neighborhood dispute resolution centers also help families resolve disputes. Such centers are numerous in large cities but may be relatively rare in other areas of the country. A referral list of local ADR programs may be obtained by writing the ABA Section on Dispute Resolution at 1800 M St., NW, Washington DC, 20036.

What Happens If We Can't Agree?

If you cannot agree on the terms of your divorce, it will go forward as a contested court case. (This is true whether the matter is in a fault or no-fault state.) The following are the typical steps in a contested divorce:

The Spouses Separate. A separation occurs when you cease to live together as husband and wife. (This is not the same thing as a judgment of legal separation. See below.) It does not necessarily mean that you have to be living in different residences. Often, finances force people to continue to live in the same house. But it does mean that you have expressed the intent or acted as if you no longer intend to remain in the marriage relationship.

The date of separation is important. For example, in community property states such as California, once parties separate, each of the spouse's individual earnings are considered their separate property rather than community property. Thus, if a salesman husband makes a sale and earns a $10,000 commission after his wife agree to live separate and apart, that money could be considered his and his alone. On the other hand, if it was earned before separation and placed in a bank, both spouses would be entitled to one-half.

> Janet and Steven were unhappily married. Janet decided she wanted to leave for a while and sort things out. She told Steven that she was going to visit her sister for a six week stay. Neither party took any other action. Under the law the parties were not separated because neither had expressed by word or deed that they intended thereafter to live separate and apart from the marriage.
>
> Jake and Helen were also unhappily married. Jake and Helen agreed that they would get a divorce when their finances were in better shape. Jake moved into the guest room. Jake and Helen stopped having sexual relations. Both opened separate bank accounts and divided their small savings account. The parties were separated even though they lived in the same house.

The Divorce Action Is Filed. In order to obtain a divorce, one of you will have to formally file for divorce in court. This is done by filling out a court form, often called the *petition* or *complaint*, handing it to the court clerk who will open up a court case, and paying a filing fee.

The petition for divorce will state the grounds for divorce, name the children of the marriage, ask for custody or visitation, list the property the petitioner contends is marital or separate, and request permanent court orders for things such as alimony and attorneys' fees. That document will then be legally served on your spouse who will usually have 30 days to file a response or answer.

An Answer or Response is Given. Once your spouse is served with divorce papers, he or she has the right to respond to the court. This is done by filing a document with the court called an *answer* or *response*. The answer allows your spouse to present the same type of information and requests as are contained in the petition.

If the case is going to be contested, it is important for the responding spouse to file the answer within the time permitted by law, usually 30 days. Failure to file an answer can result in a *default* being taken. If a default is taken, your spouse loses his or her right to appear in court and present their side of the case. (If the spouses are trying to settle the case, they can agree to waive the time period during settlement discussions. *Such agreements should always be in writing.*)

Temporary Court Orders Are Obtained. In most contested cases, one of the parties (or both) will ask the divorce court to issue temporary orders, pending the divorce. For example, the court may be asked to issue orders:

- Establishing temporary child custody.
- Setting levels of temporary child support and/or alimony.
- Issuing injunctions to prevent violence, grant exclusive use of the residence to one of the parties, prohibit either party from removing the minor children of the marriage from the state, preserve marital assets and maintain insurance policies.
- Requiring one side to pay the other's attorney's fees.

These and other pre-trial orders can be important. They create a discipline that prevents fights and arguments over things such as who pays what bill or who has the children on Saturday night. Temporary orders are obtained when one party files a court proceeding usually called an *order to show cause* (OSC). An order to show cause is an adversary proceeding where both sides have the opportunity to present their requests and evidence to support their requests. (The OSC hearing may be handled by way of a formal court hearing or in a chambers conference with the judge, depending on how congested the court calendar is.) An order to show cause is not the divorce. It does not permanently divide marital property, establish custody or resolve the long-term issues between the parties.

Discovery Is Conducted. In the months that pass between the answer being filed and the divorce trial, both sides will be allowed to "discover" the facts and evidence in possession of the other. This is a process known as *discovery.* Depositions may be taken (testimony under penalty of perjury in a lawyer's office), interrogatories may be propounded (written questions that must be answered in writing under penalty of perjury), bank records, pension information and other financial documents may be subpoenaed from the litigants and third parties. Expert witnesses, such as psychologists in a child custody case, accountants, or actuaries, may be hired by one of the parties and examined in deposition by the other. Discovery may be light in cases involving a small amount of property and relatively few issues, to extensive, complicated and expensive in cases involving a lot of money and property or contentious issues of custody and visitation.

A Settlement Conference Takes Place. Throughout the case the parties (or their lawyers) may engage in settlement discussions. If the matter has not settled as the date for trial approaches, the court will order the parties to sit down with a judge or other third party to try to resolve all contested issues. This is known as a *mandatory settlement conference*. At the conference, both parties will present legal briefs to the settlement judge or officer, stating what orders they desire and the legal basis for the requests. At that point, the settlement judge will give an opinion as to the merits and demerits of each side's case and will offer settlement recommendations. A good settlement judge will figuratively "knock heads" trying to get the parties to agree to resolve the case. However, the settlement conference is not a trial. The judge cannot order the case settled.

A Marital Settlement Agreement Is Written. Whenever the case settles, whether before the petition is filed, during discovery, at the settlement conference or even during trial, the agreement of the parties will be set down in a written contract known as a *marital settlement agreement*. The marital settlement agreement, as mentioned earlier in this book, is a contract between the parties that settles all issues in the divorce, e.g., dividing property, establishing custody and visitation, setting support levels, etc. This agreement will also become the basis for the divorce judgment and the matter can then proceed as an uncontested divorce.

The Parties Go to Trial. If the parties cannot settle every issue in their case (some cases are partially settled by the time of trial), the matter will be decided by a judge after a formal trial. At the trial, the parties will each present evidence. For example, if the issue that is being contested is the level of alimony, both sides will offer evidence about the earnings and earning abilities of the other. If the case is a custody case, both will present evidence relevant to which parent will best provide for the welfare of the children. After all of the evidence has been presented and argued, the court will decide the case and make the decisions which will be set forth in the divorce decree.

The Divorce Decree Is Given. The divorce judgment will grant a divorce and will formally divide the property, set alimony child custody and visitation, establish child support, and otherwise resolve all issues in the divorce. Once the decree is finalized (the length of this process varies from state to state), the marriage will be legally terminated and both parties are free to remarry.

One or Both Parties May Appeal. If one of the parties believes the judge did not follow the law or made a material mistake, an appeal can be filed. An appeal is a review process wherein the entire trial is looked at by a panel of judges to make sure the case was resolved correctly. Appeals are expensive. Lawyers must usually be hired and transcripts of the trial must be paid for and filed with the appeals court. Few appeals in divorce cases are successful since the trial judge is given broad discretion in making decisions.

As can be seen, divorce cases can be simple and relatively easily handled or complex and time consuming, requiring you to spend thousands of dollars on attorneys and months of your life fighting it out in litigation. However, many cases that are contested, need not have been, and increasingly, the courts are trying to help people settle their cases so that they don't clog courts and further disrupt family relations through the bitterness that an adversarial divorce often brings.

ANNULMENT

An *annulment* is a court order declaring that a marriage never legally existed. The grounds for an annulment are described in Chapter 1.

The process of obtaining an annulment is similar to that of obtaining a divorce. A petition or complaint is filed with the court requesting an annulment (or a judgment of nullity as it is often called) and setting forth the alleged grounds. Thereafter, the case will proceed much like a divorce case. There is no such thing as a no-fault annulment since you have to prove you have the right to have the marriage voided. (If you can't prove grounds, you will have to get a divorce to terminate your marriage.)

If you obtain an annulment shortly after the marriage ceremony, there will be few property or support issues for the court to decide. However, if the marriage which is annulled was of long duration, there may be decisions for the court to make regarding issues such as property disposition and children.

Here is a general overview of the way these issues are decided:

Alimony. Temporary alimony may be awarded while a suit for nullity plays itself out in the court. However, if the annulment is granted, permanent alimony will not be awarded since the couple were never legally husband and wife. In long-term relationships, some courts will attempt to provide compensation to a partner who would have been entitled to alimony had the marriage been valid, based on an "implied partnership" or "value of services rendered" theory.

Children. Custody and visitation rights are not based on the existence of a marriage but on the best interests of the child. A judgment of nullity will not affect this standard. The obligations of child support will also not be affected by an annulment.

Property Division. If property has been obtained during the annulled marriage, most courts will treat such property as they would marital property in a divorce. Other courts apply other criteria, such as the "needs of the spouse," the length of time of the relationship and other principles of fairness and equity.

Attorneys' Fees. The court is usually free to award one party the cost of their attorneys' fees in annulment cases.

Annulments are relatively rare. However, in some cases the rights or obligations of the parties can be significantly affected by obtaining an annulment rather than a divorce. For that reason, some annulment cases are hotly contested, with one spouse seeking a judgment of nullity and the other requesting a divorce.

LEGAL SEPARATION

Some married couples whose marriage has broken down, whether for religious reasons, practical business considerations or personal preference, decide to seek a judgment for *legal separation* rather than obtain a divorce. (Some states call this *separate maintenance.*) Such action is permitted in all states.

A suit for legal separation is handled in the exact same manner as a divorce and the same laws apply. The court will be asked to divide the marital property, establish child custody and set levels of child support and/or alimony. The process of going to court is the same, as is the ability of the parties to settle their case and proceed based on a marital settlement agreement.

The only difference between a legal separation and a divorce is that in a legal separation, the parties legally remain husband and wife. They are not free to remarry and they remain free to take advantage of any business or tax benefits that accrue, such as filing a joint tax return, because of their continuing legal status of being married.

If parties who are legally separated want a divorce they can obtain it. However, they will probably have to file a new case. If the parties have maintained separate households, the divorce case will go quickly since the only issue to resolve will be the termination of the marriage.

DEATH

In traditional marriage ceremonies, the bride and groom promise to remain together "until death do us part." Despite the depressing divorce statistics, death remains the number one cause for the termination of marriages.

The death of a spouse automatically ends the marriage. No formal action needs to be taken. However, there are steps that a widowed spouse should take:

Transfer Joint Property Into Your Own Name

As you will recall from the discussion in Chapter 2, property held in joint tenancy automatically becomes the sole property of the surviving joint tenant. Still, the surviving spouse will have to take action to have the titles formally changed. Thus, deeds to property, bank accounts, stock accounts, titles of ownership and other such documents will have to be changed to reflect the death of the joint tenant.

Probate the Estate

The affairs of the deceased may or may not have to be probated. If all of the property was held jointly by the spouses, probate will not be necessary. However, if the deceased spouse had substantial separate property, probate may be necessary.*

Pay Taxes

There may or may not be a tax consequence to the death of a spouse. If separate property exceeded $600,000, the federal government may require the payment of an estate tax. States may or may not charge inheritance taxes. Income taxes will also have to be filed when they are due, reflecting any earnings by the decedent during the tax year.

---

* For more information on probate and estate taxes, see HALT's book, *Probate: Settling an Estate* by Kay Ostberg in Association with HALT, Random House, 1990. $8.95.

Apply for Benefits

The death of a spouse may give the survivor certain rights or benefits. For example:

Life Insurance. If the deceased spouse's life was insured, a claim should be made promptly. You will need to contact the life insurance company and fill out the form completely. Be sure you have a certified copy of the death certificate. (Funeral directors will usually provide that service for little cost.)

Be certain you make a claim for all life insurance benefits to which you are entitled. For example, if the death was caused by an injury or illness that occurred on the job, a workers compensation claim should be made. Similarly, many employers, unions and fraternal organizations offer small term life insurance policies to their employees and/or members. Also, if the spouse who has died held credit cards, see if the company offered a life insurance benefit as a benefit of membership.

Social Security. Social Security has several benefits that a widowed person may qualify to receive. One is the survivor's benefit. This payment pays monthly benefits to the minor children of deceased workers and in some cases their widowed spouses. There is also a death benefit to help defray funeral expenses.

A Wrongful Death Suit. If the death was caused by the negligence of another, a surviving spouse and the children of the deceased may have a right to be compensated for the financial and emotional losses caused by the death. This is known as a *wrongful death* action. A personal injury attorney can give you more details. Be sure to ask for a free consultation.

8

PROPERTY DIVISION, ALIMONY & ATTORNEYS

When a court dissolves a marriage, it must make many substantive decisions that can have a substantial impact on the future lives and prospects of the divorcing couple.

One of the court's big jobs is to divide the property that has been obtained during the marriage. This chapter will describe the property that is considered part of the marital estate and the kinds of property that is subject to division by the divorce court. The differing methods of dividing property will also be described. In addition, the issue of what happens to the marital debts will be addressed.

Alimony is also a key issue in many divorces. Where once courts granted women alimony as a matter of routine, most states are now reluctant to award significant spousal support to either party, expecting both to get out into the world and work. How this operates and the exceptions to this general rule will be described, as will the tax consequences of alimony.

Finally, the chapter will end with a discussion of attorneys. How do lawyers get paid? Who is responsible? And what are the "court costs" associated with a divorce trial?

DIVISION OF PROPERTY

As you will recall from the discussion in Chapter 2, there are two principal ways in which states establish the property rights of married couples: separate property principles and community property principles. Separate property states presume that the spouse who holds title to property, whether it is a deed, a bank account or other asset obtained through his or her personal earnings during the marriage, owns it as his or her separate property. Community property rules, on the other hand, hold that all property obtained during the marriage is presumed to be owned equally by the spouses as their community property.

During a marriage, these two approaches make for drastically differing rules concerning management and control of the property. However, once the parties decide to divorce, these differences blur. In fact, while there are differences in the manner in which separate property states and community property states divide marital assets, these differences are growing increasingly small.

Division of Property in Separate Property States

At one time, separate property in separate property states would simply be awarded to the spouse who owned it. Since property was usually obtained through the earnings of the husband and put into his name, strict adherence to this policy often left the "non-earning" wife up poverty creek without any property to call her own. Because this worked such a hardship, the rules of dividing property upon divorce have been softened in most jurisdictions.

Today, courts in separate property states divide property so as to achieve an "equitable distribution" of property. This has been accomplished by creating a concept known as marital property. Marital property is now subject to division by the court on the theory that marriage is a shared enterprise. At one time, this division could be affected by the concept of "fault" but generally, that is no longer true. How does a court determine what an "equitable distribution" should be?

The Court Identifies Marital Property. Each state's laws will define property that can be considered "marital" and that which is to be considered the separate property of the spouse who owns it. *Only that property considered marital is subject to property division.* Thus, if a couple bought a house during the marriage, that would probably be considered marital property. So too would be pension rights earned during the marriage, as well as furniture, investments and automobiles.

The Court Identifies Separate Property. Some property will not be considered marital property and will not be divided by the court. (This property is still called separate property.) Separate property is usually defined as:

- Property owned before marriage.
- Property obtained by a spouse in his or her name alone by gift, inheritance or bequest (Gifts and bequests given to both spouses will be considered marital.)
- Property excluded from becoming marital property by a valid premarital contract.

Separate property may change status to that of marital property by the actions of the couple, such as commingling it with marital assets or changing title into the name of both spouses, or by having it paid for by marital assets.

Michelle and Adam were engaged. Adam purchased a home in his own name just before the wedding. The house was paid off over a period of thirty years. With the exception of a $5,000 down payment, all mortgage payments, taxes, homeowner's insurance premiums, maintenance and repairs were paid from the earnings of both spouses.

When Adam and Michelle divorced, Adam tried to claim that the house was his separate property because title was held in his name and because he purchased the house before the marriage. The judge ruled the house was marital property because almost all of the money to pay for and support the house came from marital assets. Thus the house was subject to division by the court even though title was in Adam's name alone.

Dividing the Marital Property

There are no fixed rules as to how the property is to be divided—only that the division be "just" or "reasonable." Of course, what is reasonable to one person may be tyranny to another. However, someone has to make the decision, and so the trial court judge is given broad latitude in the manner and method by which he or she accomplishes a fair division. In fact, it is not unusual for both parties to be unhappy with the court's decision. (For this reason, going to trial can be a gamble. Thus, reaching a fair settlement is to be preferred to litigation.) Marital misconduct is no longer taken into account when dividing the property.

Among the factors that a judge will look at when determining what is a fair division, are the following:

- The role of each spouse in obtaining the property to be divided.
- The respective needs of the spouses.
- The relative abilities of the spouses to obtain employment.
- The duration of the marriage.
- The value of each spouse's separate property.

The judge will then divide the property, usually giving each partner approximately half the value.

That does not mean that each piece of property must be divided in two. Rather, the court can order one party to pay the other for one-half the value, either in lump sum or in payments, or can give some property to one spouse and other items of similar value to the other spouse. Again, the judge has broad latitude and his or her decisions can rarely be successfully challenged on appeal.

Dividing Property in Community Property States

The process of dividing the property in community property states is similar to that now performed in separate property states. (It should be; the concept of marital property has been borrowed from community property rules.) First, the property that is deemed community must be identified. Likewise, inherited property, gifts and property set aside by contract as the separate property of one spouse will not be divided since it is separate, not community property. Then the court must divide all community property *equally* between the spouses. Considerations such as marital fault and the relative involvement of the respective spouses in obtaining the property are irrelevant. However, the judge has discretion about the manner in which the property will be divided, so long as the division is equal.

Here is an example of how a property division might differ between a community and separate property state in a hypothetical marriage where the couple has property valued at $262,000:

Debra and David lived in a separate property state. There were four marital assets to the marriage: a house worth $120,000; two cars, a Toyota worth $6,000 and a BMW worth $36,000; and David's pension, worth $100,000. The house payment was $450 a month. David earned $100,000 a year. Debra was a homemaker who worked part-time and earned $12,000 a year. She and David had agreed she would be caring for the couple's two young children.

The court divided the marital assets as follows:

DEBRA		**DAVID**	
The house–value	$120,000	The pension–value	$100,000
The Toyota–value	$6,000	The BMW–value	$36,000
Total Value:	$126,000		$136,000

The fact that David receives property worth $10,000 more than his wife does not prevent the court from making this division, especially since it gives the house to the wife with a low-payment mortgage.

Had David and Debra lived in a community property state, the judge could have made the same division but would have been compelled to further order David to pay Debra $5,000 to equalize the division of all property at exactly $131,000 each.

It is important to emphasize that neither a court in a separate property state or a community property state would necessarily divide the assets "in kind" as occurred in this illustration. For example, the house could have been ordered sold and the proceeds divided, with Debra receiving her share of David's pension when he started to receive payments. Or, David could have been given the house and pension and been ordered to pay Debra her share immediately in cash. The point is this: trial courts have broad discretion in dividing property, so long as it is fair and just in separate property states and an equal division in community property states.

ISSUES TO WATCH OUT FOR

Some issues involved with dividing property are relatively simple. For example, the value of real property (i.e., land or house) can be proven by having it professionally appraised. Similarly, the value of automobles, furniture and other such "non-unique" properties rarely cause significant controversy.

There are, however, areas that continue to dog the courts, making it difficult to divide property and interfering with easy settlements between the parties. These issues include:

Who Gets to Keep the House?

Often, the major asset of a marriage is the house. That leaves divorcing parties fighting about whether it will be sold and the proceeds divided or whether the party with custody will be able to live in the house until the children reach adulthood. The courts will decide this on a case-by-case basis, often allowing a custodial parent to stay in the house for a few years if the payments are low and it is deemed in the best interests of the children that they not be forced to move. However, few courts will make a spouse wait many years before receiving his or her share of the value of the house, since that money is often required to buy another home and otherwise start over again.

The Value of a Business

Businesses can be hard to appraise, especially when its worth primarily consists of goodwill. Goodwill is an intangible asset. For example, a self-employed business consultant may have little in the way of tangible business assets such as inventory or machinery but may make $300,000 a year because of the faith his customers repose in him. In other words, he is the business—the business is him. It cannot be sold for great value because without the consultant to serve the clients, there will be no business. Yet, so long as he is doing business, the enterprise brings in a lot of money. So, what is it worth? The courts have wrestled with the problem for years, confusing themselves and in the process, lawyers who try to apply the law.

The Value of a Professional License

What should happen when one spouse puts his or her mate through law or medical school only to face a divorce when the educational goal has been attained and the years of hard work will begin to pay off financially? A few state courts have ruled that a professional license is "property" that can be valued and distributed as any other marital asset. For example, in New York, a court of appeals held that a husband's license to practice medicine was subject to distribution by the court. Other states have refused to declare licenses as marital property, but have held that the efforts (e.g., maintaining a household or financially supporting a spouse who is attending school) of the nonlicensed spouse should be considered when determining levels of alimony.

Tax Consequences

Tax consequences can be taken into account by courts when they divide property. However, the consequences must be immediate and pending. They cannot be speculative. One tax consequence that some divorcing people overlook is the capital gains tax problem. A capital gains tax is a tax based on the increase in value of an asset. Thus, if a house is purchased for $100,000 and sold for $200,000, the "gain" is $100,000, an amount which would be subject to tax. (Capital gains taxes on residential property can be deferred if the gain money is used to buy new residential property. For more details, ask your accountant.) In a divorce, if one spouse is "bought out" of an asset such as a house, or stocks, and if the price that is paid represents a "gain," a tax consequence may occur. Thus, before agreeing to any buy-out type of settlement, make sure you understand all of the potential tax consequences.

Debts

Debts, like assets, are subject to division. In community property states, "community debts,"—that is, debts incurred during the marriage—must be equally divided by the court. (The divorcing spouses can make other arrangements in a settlement.) The apportionment of debts will also be considered in determining the equitable division of property in a separate property state.

Pensions

Pensions earned during a marriage are community or marital property, subject to division by the court. If part of the pension was earned during the marriage and part outside the marriage, the value that was earned during marriage is subject to the court's power to divide the property.

If the pension is being received at the time of the divorce, dividing it may be relatively easy. But what if the pension is not yet payable? The courts may determine the marital value (using expert witnesses such as accountants or actuaries to determine the dollar worth of the plan) and divide that. Or, they may order the spouse who receives the pension to pay his former spouse her marital share, or the pension may be awarded to the receiving spouse and other property awarded to the nonreceiving spouse as a form of equalizing the division or making it fair. Sometimes, the pension is named as a party to the divorce so that the court can order the pension plan to pay the nonpensioned spouse directly.

As you can see, dividing property is not as easy in practice as it may at first appear on paper. Issues such as these and others can lead to divorce litigation that is protracted, bitter and hotly contested. That is why mediation with an expert in these issues can be very important in saving money, time and emotional bitterness. If you have any further questions, or wish to learn more about the law in your state as it applies to specific types of property, go to your local law library and look at a law encyclopedia. You can also usually receive a low-cost or free consultation from a family lawyer.

ALIMONY

Alimony, or *spousal support* as it is now sometimes called, is a court order requiring one divorcing party, almost always but not exclusively the husband, to help support the other. Alimony is designed to do many things:

- Keep the wife from becoming a dependent of the state.
- Maintain the wife's accustomed lifestyle in affluent family situations where the marriage is a long one.
- Compensate the wife for her services during the marriage.
- Make up for unequal distribution of property in separate property states (a consideration that has become less important with the inception of the concept of marital property—see above).

Many of the legal concepts that govern alimony were created in a more traditional time when the husband worked and the wife served her family as homemaker, sacrificing career prospects to stay at home and take care of the kids.

With strict gender roles eroding and women increasingly finding a place in the workforce, alimony is now looked on with disfavor in most jurisdictions. In many cases, alimony awards are smaller and for a shorter duration than they used to be. Sometimes, no alimony is awarded at all in cases that would have resulted in such payments only a few years ago.

There are various reasons cited for the growing hostility to alimony:

- Women enjoy career opportunities that were unheard of just twenty years ago. (On occasion, this leads to the woman paying alimony, such as television journalist Joan Lunden.)
- Property divisions are more fair than was once the case.
- Alimony is look upon by some as reverse sexism.
- A man's ability to pay is lower than it used to be, especially if he must also pay child support.

Still, in longer marriages where the wife served the relationship in the traditional role of "homemaker and wife," alimony remains likely to be awarded. Also, if one of the spouses is severely ill or disabled, alimony may also be awarded even if the marriage was short. However, in shorter marriages, alimony is either not awarded or if it is ordered it will be for a very brief duration.

The following are the factors the court considers when deciding to award alimony:

- The length of the marriage.
- The needs of the supported spouse.
- Special circumstances, such as ill health or the fact that the supported spouse gave up a career after marriage.
- The ability of the supporting spouse to pay alimony.
- Alimony as reimbursement, such as when a wife's efforts helped her husband obtain a professional license.
- Occasionally, marital fault in states that permit fault divorce, although to a far less extent than was once the case.

An award of alimony will often be established in a step-down form. For example, if the supported spouse needs education or job training to better be able to earn a living, the award may begin at a higher level and "step-down" after a period of time when it is presumed the wife will be able to work. The same may hold true if the wife has been given custody of small children. Other cases permit a "jurisdictional award" of alimony. In a jurisdictional award, the court will not order the husband to pay alimony but will reserve jurisdiction (power) to award it in the future if the wife can show need.

Alimony is usually paid in periodic payments. However, there can be a lump sum payment or alimony ordered in the form of paying third parties. Also, a court order requiring the payer of alimony to pay the recipient's attorney's fees is usually considered a form of alimony.

The manner in which alimony is paid can be important. Unlike child support payments, *alimony is usually an income taxable event.* The money is usually taxable to the supported spouse and deductible from the taxes of the paying spouse. (Thus, if you receive alimony, be sure and set some money aside to pay income taxes.) However, the parties may be able to agree that the payments will not be treated as taxable if the divorce decree specifies that the alimony will not be considered part of the gross income of the recipient and tax-deductible by the payer.

Alimony terminates on the remarriage of the supported spouse, the death of either party, on order of court, or on the date the court judgment states that its jurisdiction (power) to award alimony ceases. (The court will often place a term in the divorce decree setting a date on which the court's jurisdiction to award alimony ceases. Once jurisdiction ends, the court loses the legal power to award it regardless of hardship or changed circumstances.) Like child support, alimony can be modified up · or down upon a showing of changed circumstances.

Alimony can be enforced in the same ways as child support can—i.e., through contempt proceedings, wage garnishment, etc. Wage assignment may or may not be available, depending on the laws of your state. (See Chapter 10 for more on enforcing support orders.) Like child support, back alimony is not dischargable in bankruptcy.

ATTORNEYS AND DIVORCE

Finally, we come to the role of attorneys in a divorce. One of the major goals of the legal reform movement is to permit people to handle more of their legal problems without having to retain an attorney. Many people handle divorces without using a lawyer. Others decide they should retain attorneys to represent them. If you decide to hire a lawyer to help you, keep the following considerations in mind:

Only Hire a Lawyer with Expertise in Divorce Law. A lawyer who normally handles personal injury law or corporate matters will not be of much use in a contested divorce since he or she may have little better understanding of divorce law than you. (Some states allow divorce lawyers to become certified specialists. If you have a complex case or a matter in which a lot of money is involved, you may wish to consider hiring such a specialist.)

Always Have a Written Agreement. Do not hire a lawyer based on an oral agreement. That only leads to misunderstandings. Instead, be sure the fee agreement (called a retainer agreement) is in writing and that you understand all of its terms.

Divorce Lawyers usually Charge "By the Hour." That means you are going to have to keep a sharp eye on the bill. Thus, do not accept a bill that reads, "fees for services rendered." Rather, insist on a detailed monthly billing statement. If you find a mistake or there is a charge you don't understand, bring it to the attention of your lawyer.

Don't Be Passive. Just because you have a lawyer, that doesn't mean you do not have a job to do. You should ask questions and read books so as to better understand the law and the process. You—not you lawyer—should make the ultimate decisions about how to proceed with your case. After all, it's your life and your future that is at stake, not your lawyer's.

Here are some sample questions you will want to ask your lawyer. You may also want to add more of your own.[*]

- How long will my case take?
- What will be happening step-by-step?
- What is your best estimate of the fees I will be charged?
- How much will the *costs* be? (Costs are all "out-of-pocket" expenses that are incurred to support the litigation. Examples are court filing fees and paying court reporters for deposition transcription services. Costs can mount into the thousands of dollars in contested cases.)
- Will I be asked to pay the other sides attorneys' fees? Can I have my spouse pay my attorneys' fees?
- Can I get protective orders? For example, if you are being threatened with or have been subjected to violence, your attorney should be able to get a restraining order within a day or two.

---

[*] For more information on working with a lawyer, see *Using a Lawyer . . . And What to Do If Things Go Wrong,* by Kay Ostberg in Association with HALT, Random House. 1990. $8.95.

- After describing what you want out of the divorce, e.g., by way of property division, custody and support, ask: Can this be done? If not, why not? If so, what are the problems we face in getting what I want?
- How much support should I ask for (or offer to pay)?
- How can I be sure that I get my visitation, child support, alimony, etc.?

Ask about whatever you don't understand or think you may not understand. Also, listen to what the lawyer says. Part of his or her job is to educate you about what you will be going through. Remember, you have the *right* to answers. Never accept a condescending answer such as, "It's too complicated, you wouldn't understand." And especially don't accept, "Trust me, it's all under control."

That concludes our discussion of divorce and divorce law. Due to the general nature of this book, which is addressed to a national audience, every detail of the law in every state has not been covered. Thus, if you want to find out "what will happen" in your specific case, research the law in your state in your local law library or ask an attorney. You can also turn to Appendix 4 (Bibliography) for a listing of additional resources.

9

CUSTODY &
VISITATION

"Who gets custody of the kids?" That question is asked hundreds of thousands of times a year by well-meaning parents who are divorcing or ceasing to live together. (More than a decade ago, the government published statistics indicating that in 32 states that were surveyed, more than 1 million children were members of divorcing families each year. And that doesn't include parents who separate or who are not married.) Of all of the issues faced in family law courts, answering this question is the most difficult and often the most heart-wrenching—and emotionally draining—both for the parents and their children.

It is not surprising that the courts don't like to make this decision, preferring instead that parents work out the issue in mediation. (Most child custody and visitation disputes must go through mediation, called conciliation court, before a court will agree to decide the issue.) The courts also hope that mediation will help prevent vindictive parents from bringing a custody or visitation case as a form of punishment of an ex-spouse rather than as a way to serve the best interests of the children. Also, courts and family experts have recognized that in most situations it is in the best interest of the children to have ongoing and meaningful contact with both parents. Thus, the concept of joint custody has been pioneered, along with a tendency to award custody to that parent who will best foster a healthy relationship between the other parent and the children.

This chapter will answer the most fundamental questions parents ask concerning issues of child custody and its twin issue, visitation. Among the questions that will be answered are: What does "custody" mean? How is the decision made? What is joint custody? What are the rights of the parent who does not get custody? How can visitation rights be enforced? What happens if a custodial parent wants to move away from the area where the visiting parent lives? And what is being done to prevent child stealing by parents?

CHILD CUSTODY

Who Has Custody of Children When There Is No Court Order?

Both parents have co-equal rights to custody of their children, absent a court order giving custody to one or the other. What does this mean? It means that both parents have joint decision making rights concerning their children and their upbringing. Even if the parents do not agree, absent child abuse or neglect, the courts will not involve themselves, as the area is considered too private and personal for the law to intervene. Thus, it is not possible to go to court and ask a judge to decide a decision about child-rearing when the family is intact.

What Is the Meaning of "Custody"?

When parents are not going to live together in a single household, courts are frequently requested to decide which parent has the right to *custody*. (This is true whether the parents are married and getting a divorce or were never married and are contesting custody.) Depending on where you live, you may be awarded *legal custody* and or *physical custody* of your child(ren). Some states allow *joint custody* where both parents share physcial and legal custody of their children. However, most states still award legal and physical custody to one parent (usually the mother) and visitation rights to the other parent.

If awarded legal custody in a divorce or paternity action, you

have the right to make decisions regarding your children in the
following areas:

- Education
- Health care
- Religious upbringing
- Choice of residence address (usually with the custodial
  parent)
- Parental control over your children's lives
- The everyday matters parents decide regarding the up-
  bringing of children

Once a court has awarded custody to one parent, that does
not mean the noncustodial parent loses the right to be involved
in these important issues. For example, noncustodial parents
(except in unusual circumstances, such as where violence is
threatened) have the right to discuss their children's education
with teachers, their health with doctors, and religious beliefs
with clergy. In fact, child-rearing experts say that it is in the best
interest of the child's continuing relationship of the parents, for
both parents to continue to be intimately involved with all
aspects of rearing their children, regardless of formal custody
orders.

Can the Parents Agree to Custody?

Thankfully, most child custody decisions are reached by
agreement between the parents. A court will usually follow the
desires of the parents. However, the court does not have to
accept the agreement if it believes the best interests of the
children are not served.

Courts, often called conciliation courts, try to help parents
achieve agreement by offering mediation services.

How Is Custody Determined?

In most cases, parents agree to issues of custody and visitation
and those decisions are ratified by the court. If the parties cannot
agree and if mediation fails, a trial will be held and the court will
make the choice.

Believe it or not, at one time, the father was the one with the primary right to custody upon divorce. (This wasn't true if the child was born "out of wedlock.") Later, the mother became the person with the primary right to custody, especially of younger children (the *tender years doctrine*). Then, an increasing number of fathers began to actively seek custody and the law changed again. Today, at least in theory, both parents come before the court equal in the eyes of the law and the custody decision will be based not on gender but on the "best interests of the child."

How Are the Best Interests of the Child Determined?

Divorcing parents have two choices: They can either agree beforehand on custody and visitation—perhaps with the assistance of mediation—or they can fight it out in court and let a judge decide. Child custody fights are some of the most expensive, divisive and emotionally devastating actions that lawyers, litigants and judges face. Simply put, they are awful and can cause emotional, financial and mental distress for all parties involved. However, sometimes they are necessary. If you are going through a divorce and can't reach agreement on custody, and you decide to make a fight of it, the following are some of the issues that will be looked at by a court:

Who Has Been the Primary Care-Giver? The parent who can prove that they have been most involved in raising the child will argue that they have been the primary care-giver and it is in the best interests of the child that this status quo be continued. The court will seek answers to questions such as:

- Who gets the children ready for school?
- Who is most involved with the children's school and teachers?
- Who usually provides care when the child is ill?
- Who shops with the child?
- Who spends the most quality time with the child?
- Who does the child look to for help when he or she is hurt or in trouble?

In short, which parent has been the primary nurturer with the most profound parent/child relationship?

With Whom Does the Child Want to Live? The desires of older children (generally, age 12 and up) will be given great weight by a court. (Children will usually be asked their opinions in private in the judge's chambers, an experience your child is unlikely to soon forget. Few children relish having to choose between two parents they love.) Younger children are deemed too young and immature to express an opinion. However, if a court determines that a child has been pressured or coerced into making a choice, the coercing parent may find that their unethical tactic backfires. The court does not have to accept the child's choice if it is not deemed in the best interests of the child.

What Are the Opinions of the "Experts?" Courts usually rely heavily on experts such as psychologists and family counselors to reach an opinion as to the best interests of the children. Courts will often assign social workers and/or psychologists to investigate the family circumstances and emotional state of each family member and then write a recommendation regarding the custody choice. This means that your private lives will be exposed and judged in court. These reports will compare and contrast the quality and depth of the personal interaction between each parent and child, and will address such issues as each litigant's parenting skills, living arrangements, whether a child will have to leave a neighborhood or school, the desires of the child, etc. In fact, if it comes to this, each parent will often hire their own experts (at great expense) and have them testify in court on these issues. Soon, the trial has become a battle of the experts with the life and parenting skills of each parent subject to attack and distortion.

How Has each Parent Behaved? At one time, a parent deemed "immoral" would lose custody. Thus, in earlier times, a parent who had committed adultery would often lose custody because he or she had acted improperly. Today, the issue of "morality" is no longer relevant in and of itself. However, that doesn't mean that mud isn't thrown. The conduct of the parents will be looked at if it may adversely impact the well-being of the child, and some courts allow a very wide latitude. (Child custody fights are sometimes used by hurt and angry parents to bring "fault" back into the divorce process.) Here are some illustrations based on actual cases:

Yvonne and Mark separated and filed for divorce. Yvonne began to date Harry. Harry and Yvonne limited their intimate activities to times when the children were visiting their father and acted as "friends" when the children were present. When, in the custody case, Mark attempted to bring up the fact that Yvonne had a boyfriend, the judge did not care because the relationship had been handled with maturity and discretion and with sensitivity to the feelings of the children.

Carl and Eileen also separated and filed for divorce. Eileen's boyfriend moved into the home immediately after Carl left and slept with Eileen. This upset the children who began to act badly in school and get bad grades on tests. The youngest child also began to wet the bed. The court appointed psychologist reported that the childrens' problems were caused by their reaction to their mother's new relationship. The court took this evidence into account when making the custody decision because Eileen's private life adversely impacted the well-being of her children.

Troy and Susan separated and filed for divorce. Troy began to date Theresa. The children told their mother that when they stayed with their father, he and Theresa could be seen naked in their bed together and that they could be heard making love. This upset the children very much, who threatened to run away rather than live with their father. The court took evidence on the issue as it related to the children's emotional welfare.

Andrew and Patty were divorced. Andrew was living with Nancy. The children and Nancy loved each other and got along well. Patty told the court she wanted the children because she claimed it was harmful for them to see their father with another woman who was not his wife. Andrew proved that the children and Nancy got along well and that Nancy would be home for the children when they came home from school. On the other hand, Patty worked all day and would have to put the children in day care. Moreover, her work schedule would force her to get the children up at six in the morning everyday to go to day care before school started. The court ruled in favor of Andrew because he could provide a more stable home.

Some readers may think that these case decisions were designed to punish parental lifestyles or discriminate against single women. But that is not how the court would see it. Rather than judging the morality of the parties, the court would state that it was merely seeking to serve the best interests of the *children*—not the parents—even if the decision seems unfair to one of the parents. (For example, in the last example the single mom had done nothing wrong. After all, she *had* to work to support herself and her family. But good relationship between the children and their father's new partner, in the court's opinion, made that household a better place for the children to live.)

Is There a Religious Conflict? One of the most difficult issues courts face is that of determining religious upbringing. The courts will sometimes take into consideration the planned religious upbringing of the children. For example, if a child has been raised a Catholic and one parent intends to change the upbringing to Baptist, the court might consider the impact that would have on the child. Also, if a religion of a parent is considered "extreme" or potentially harmful, the court will consider the issue when determining custody.

Other Issues. Other issues will also be addressed, such as the parent's respective plans for raising their children, the nature and quality of each parent's relationship with the children, which parent best handles stress, which parent is most likely to promote a healthy relationship between the children and the noncustodial parent, and how has each parent dealt with issue of discipline.

As this discussion demonstrates, there are a tremendous number of factors that go into the custody decision. Each case is decided on the basis of its own merits and the individual circumstances involved.

What Is Joint Custody?

Feeling that they were being treated unfairly in custody cases, many fathers formed groups lobbied for laws in the states to encourage joint custody. (About half the states currently have laws either permitting or encouraging such custody orders.)

In a growing number of states, parents may be awarded joint legal and/or joint physical custody of their children. That means both parents get to share in parental decision-making about such things as education, medical care, and religion (if awarded joint legal custody) and both get to live with their children at predetermined times of the year (if awarded physical custody). Not all courts award joint legal and physical custody to both parents, though. Both parents may be awarded joint legal custody while one parent is awarded sole physical custody.

A joint custody arrangement is seen by mental health experts as in the best interests of children because it keeps both parents vitally involved in their children's upbringing. However, the joint custody arrangement is only meaningful when both parents work hard to get along with each other in areas involving their children and where both the mother and the father cooperate in ensuring that their children develop a strong and healthy relationship with each parent. It is also helpful for the parents to live close to each other so that the children can spend a lot of time with both their mother and their father.

If the parents end up in continual disagreements over decision-making or cannot get along well enough to make joint custody successful, one or the other will be awarded sole custody (based on the best interests of the children). When making the determination, the court may look into the reasons why the joint custody did not work. If the failure was caused by one parent's uncooperative conduct, it may award custody to the other parent.

Can a Grandparent, other Relative or a Nonparent ever Get Custody of Children? Nonparents can obtain custody of children, usually in a guardianship action, although that can occur in other proceedings such as a dependency hearing in juvenile court or in a divorce case itself.

Unless both parents agree to grant custody to a nonparent, achieving such a result will be difficult because the law prefers that children remain in the custody of biological parents. Thus, a nonparent who is seeking to take custody away from a parent faces a daunting task. In order to overcome the built-in preference for the parent, the nonparent will have to present very strong proof of the parent's unfitness due to abuse or severe neglect.

What Happens If One Parent Takes a Child to Another State?

Sometimes, one parent wants to have a child custody case heard in a different state where he or she thinks they will have a better chance of winning. That has often resulted in "child-stealing;" that is, one parent taking a child to a different state and seeking custody there. This causes severe problems for the other parent and confusion in the courts. (For example, it is not unheard of for two courts in two different states to issue two different child custody orders over the same children.)

Several steps have been taken to end the confusion and deter child-stealing. They are:

The Uniform Child Custody Jurisdiction Act. Every state has passed a law known generically as the Uniform Child Custody Jurisdiction Act (UCCJA). The UCCJA seeks to end court shopping by parents by creating the standards by which courts will decide where a child custody lawsuit shall be heard. The UCCJA seeks to ensure that the case will be heard in a locale with most *significant contacts* (the closest association) with the child. (It is presumed that a trial that takes place in the locale with the most contacts with the child will allow the court the best access to evidence required to make a custody decision in the best interests of the child.)

Here is an illustration based on a real-life case:

Maureen and Dick were married in Michigan and their son, Jay, was born in that state. The family lived in Michigan until Jay was five, when the family moved to California. The family lived in California for the next five years. Then, Maureen and Dick broke up and planned to divorce.

Both parents wanted custody. One day, Maureen took Jay to Michigan because that was where her parents lived and where she felt she could best get a new start. She filed for divorce in Michigan and obtained an order of temporary custody. Dick did not appear in court.

In the meantime, Dick had filed his own divorce action in California. He too was granted temporary custody of Jay. Maureen did not appear at that hearing.

Dick then went to Michigan and asked the Michigan court to dismiss Maureen's case and to terminate its order giving temporary custody to Maureen. He based his request on the Uniform Child Custody Jurisdiction Act and the law's requirement that the state with the closest contacts with the child and the best access to information about the child, be the state that makes the custody decision. Maureen opposed the request.

After a court hearing, Michigan granted Dick's request. Jay had lived in California for the last five years of his life. California was where Jay's doctors, teachers and friends lived, as well as his father and paternal grandmother. That was where people who had observed Dick and Maureen's parenting skills could be found. While it was true that Jay had been born in Michigan, the only contact he had with the state during the last five years, were brief visits to see his maternal grandparents. That being so, the court ruled that the child custody fight would have to be in California. Jay was placed in his father's custody based on the valid California temporary order. Maureen still wanted to fight for custody. She was allowed to do so in California.

The UCCJA also applies long after a divorce is over. Child custody and visitation orders can be modified (see below). The UCCJA states that the court that made the original order retains jurisdiction to decide future custody modifications unless the parties and child no longer have close ties to the court and the court decides to end its own power to decide the issue.

The UCCJA also tries to deter child-stealing by allowing a court that would have the power to hear a custody case to refuse to do so if the child is in the court's area of jurisdiction because the child has been wrongfully taken from another state or because the child has been taken without the consent of a person entitled to custody.

The Federal Parental Kidnapping Prevention Act. It is a felony, punishable by law in many states, for a parent to kidnap his or her child after a state with proper jurisdiction has rendered a custody decision in favor of the other parent. In such cases, the FBI can be called in to find the fugitive parent and the stolen child. Such criminal sanctions are a potent deterrent to child stealing.

There is an exception to this rule. If there is a bona-fide emergency such as child abuse or abandonment which requires the noncustodial parent to intervene to save the child, the law will not punish the taking as a criminal act. (Of course, the "stealing" parent had better be able to prove that the emergency legitimately exists. The parent may also have to show why he or she did not seek relief from the court with jurisdiction over the child custody order.)

Is There Any Way to Prevent My Former Spouse Who Has Custody of Our Children from Moving Out of State?

No court can prevent a spouse from moving out-of-state. However, they may be able to prevent children who are the subject of a custody order to be moved out of state, if the court determines that the move would not be in the best interest of the child. The key word here is "may." In order to prevent the move, the noncustodial parent would have to seek custody. Courts can issue orders preventing a custodial parent from moving out of the area without prior permission of the noncustodial parent or prior order of court. The purpose for this type of order is to give the noncustodial parent the right to object to the move and seek custody of the children before the move is a *fait accompli*. However, if the noncustodial parent is not given custody, the court will usually grant permission to make the move.

If a child is moved out of state, a joint custody arrangement or the terms of visitation may have to change to accommodate the new reality. For example, if a visiting parent saw his children every other weekend, that order may be changed to eight weeks during the summer to better allow meaningful contact between the noncustodial parent and his or her children.

VISITATION

It is the policy of the law that both parents be allowed close continuing contact with their children whenever possible. Thus, the parent who is not awarded physical custody of his or her children, will have the right to visit with the children – a right that can be enforced by court order.

Visitation orders can be general or specific. The more likely it is that the parents will be able to decide the schedule of visitation between themselves, the less likely the court is to establish a rigid formula. Thus, a court may award physical custody to one parent and "reasonable visitation" to the other, leaving the details to be worked out in a cooperative spirit between the parties themselves.

But what happens if the parties are too angry with each other or too immature to leave the decision solely in their hands? In such cases, it is in the best interests of the children for the court (or the parties by agreement) to create a detailed order that is enforceable in court. The order will often look something like this:

The court awards custody of the minor child Jacob Jones to the wife with reasonable visitation reserved to the husband, such reasonable visitation being defined as follows:

- Every other weekend from 7:00 P.M. Friday to Sunday at 7:00 P.M.
- One week each Christmas during the child's school vacation. In even numbered years, the visitation shall

take place during the 1st week. In odd numbered years, the visitation shall be during the second week.

- Three weeks each summer. Husband is to give wife one month's prior notice as to which three weeks he shall exercise this right.
- Every Father's Day.
- Every father's birthday.
- Five days every other spring vacation.
- Every other Thanksgiving.
- Any other time as the parties may mutually agree.

It is tragic that courts have to involve themselves so specifically in people's lives, but sometimes that is the only way to keep peace within a broken family and to ensure that the noncustodial parent is allowed continuing and ongoing access to his or her children.

Sometimes there is a reasonable fear that one parent might be potentially harmful or might try to steal the child during a visit. In such cases, visitation can be ordered restricted. Restricted visitation usually requires that all visits between parent and child be chaperoned by a responsible adult acceptable to the court (often a close friend or family member). In cases of unusual risk, visitation rights can be suspended altogether. Such decisions, like all custody and visitation decrees, will be made in the best interests of the child.

Grandparents sometimes complain that they are prevented from visiting their grandchildren. Some courts have made orders permitting such visitation in divorce proceedings. Others have refused, saying that grandparent visitation is a privilege, not a right.

Another issue that is frequently raised in family court is the right of a parent who is not paying child support to visit. It is a rule of law that visitation is for the welfare of the child and is not dependent on payment of child support. Thus, a parent who refuses to allow visits when the noncustodial parent is behind on child support faces the possibility of court sanction. (His or her proper course is to seek to enforce the child support order. See Chapter 10.)

Visitation orders can be enforced by the court. (In order to do so, a specific order rather than a general order should be in place.) Willful violation of visitation orders can be punished by a contempt of court order, which could lead to the jailing of the refusing parent who repeatedly refuses to follow the court's order. Moreover, many courts will take custody of children away from a parent who refuses to allow his or her children to have a meaningful relationship with the visiting parent.

MODIFICATION OF CUSTODY AND VISITATION ORDERS

A court order of custody will remain in effect until the death of the child, his or her reaching majority or further order of the court. In other words, the court retains the power to change the custody and visitation order, so long as it is in the best interests of the children.

In order to modify a custody/visitation decree, one of the parties will have to file a motion (sometimes known as an *order to show cause* motion) which petitions the court for a modification of the court order. The motion will have to demonstrate to the court through testimony and/or written declarations made under penalty of perjury that it is in the best interests of the child to make the requested change. The other parent will be given the opportunity to respond. If the request is contested, a trial may be held, after which the court will either refuse to change the court's order or will make modifications.

Parents frequently agree to make voluntary changes in custody and visitation arrangements. For example, if they wish to change custody or the terms of visitation, they can sign an agreement and prepare a court order based on the agreement to file with the court. After that, the court will sign the order which will become binding on the parties.

If you want to enter into a stipulation for custody or to modify a current custody order, go to your local law library. Ask the librarian to show you the form books which will inform you how the court stipulation should appear and which will give you the procedural details you need to follow to make sure your desires can be reduced to a formal court order. You can also hire an attorney to draft and file the document.

10

CHILD SUPPORT

An unfortunate fact of economic life is that a family cannot live as cheaply divided as it can together. Thus, after a divorce, the living standard of the entire family is often lowered and the court often finds itself in the unenviable position of having to divide a scarcity of resources. Then too, there is the problem of changing the child support order to meet changing needs of children and enforcing court orders against fathers and mothers who either refuse to make court ordered child support payments or who cannot do so due to circumstances beyond their control. These problems, when added to the issues of custody, visitation and the division of property in a divorce (see Chapters 8 and 9), keep the family law courts of the country packed to capacity.

We now turn to the issue of child support when viewed in the context of a divorce or paternity action. Just as courts must often make the crucial decision as to child custody and visitation, so too must it often determine how much child support the noncustodial parent will be ordered to pay. This chapter will describe the considerations that a court will take into account when deciding the issue of child support, whether in a divorce or a paternity case. It will also describe the methods by which child support orders are enforced by courts and how to modify an order for support. At the end of the chapter there are answers to the most common child support enforcement questions.

ESTABLISHING CHILD SUPPORT PAYMENTS

In Chapter 6, the obligation of parents to support their children was detailed. During a marriage or committed relationship, such issues are rarely a concern for the court. But when parents divorce or cease to live together with their children as a family, the courts are usually required to establish the amount of child support a noncustodial parent must pay. Like the issue of custody, this can be reached by agreement or by fighting it out in front of a judge.

The Nature of the Child Support Order

There are several parts to most child support orders. First and foremost, the paying parent will almost always be ordered to make a monthly money payment to the custodial parent. The order will typically read, in part, as follows:

> Father (name) is ordered to pay directly over to mother (name) child support of children (name) and (name), the sum of $300 per month per child for a total of $600, payable one-half on the first and one-half on the fifteenth day of each month, said payments to continue until each such child shall die, reach majority, or become emancipated, or until further order of court.

Notice the following about this portion of the child support order:

It Requires a Direct Monetary Payment to the Custodial Parent. Many paying parents resent the child support order because it is made directly to the custodial parent and not the children. Because of this, some refuse to make the payments because they see it as a form of alimony. However, this is not true. The direct payments are to be used to pay for the vital needs of the children, such as rent, food, and clothes.

The Court Retains Jurisdiction to Change the Order. A child support order is not set in concrete but is subject to change should future conditions warrant. Thus, either parent may petition the court to raise or lower support should conditions warrant (see below).

Payments Automatically Terminate when the Child Reaches Majority, Dies or Becomes Emancipated. The purpose of this language is to provide for an automatic end to the support obligation when the child reaches majority or dies. However, the issue of emancipation is often in dispute and may require a court determination. (See Chapter 6.)

Child Support Is an Enforceable Order of the Court. A child support order is as enforceable as any other court judgment or decree. Thus, a parent who is not paid child support can use each and every legal tool available to enforce the order, including wage garnishments, wage assignments, contempt-of-court decrees and seizure of the nonpayor's property by *writ of execution.*

The child support decree is not limited to an order of direct money payments to the custodial parent. Other areas of providing for the children's needs are also usually addressed. The following language is an example of a typical child support order:

As and for additional child support, father (name) is ordered to maintain his children as beneficiaries on his health and life insurance policies available through his employment. Father is further ordered to pay for one-half of all uninsured medical, dental and ophthalmological services provided for the children.

As and for additional child support, father shall pay directly to the ABC Daycare Cooperative, the full cost of afternoon after-school day care. However, should the children be enrolled in morning day care, such expenses shall be the sole responsibility of the mother.

As and for additional child support, father shall pay the round-trip plane and other reasonable costs of transporting the children for visitation with father, as provided in the visitation provisions of this order. However, during visits of two weeks or more, the father's child support payments to mother shall be reduced by $50 per month per child.

These clauses illustrate the flexible nature of child support orders and the wide latitude a court has in creating a support arrangement it deems in the best interests of the children. (The court will try to maintain the lifestyle the children enjoyed before the divorce if the parents' finances permit.) Thus, a parent can be ordered to maintain insurance for the benefit of children, pay medical bills, private school expenses, day care costs, transportation bills, music lessons and to pay or partially pay for other aspects of a child's day-to-day life, activities and upbringing. The amount of support can also be reduced should the noncustodial parent have physical custody of the children for an extended period.

How the Court Determines the Amount of Child Support

In determining an award of child support, a court will look at all relevant facts upon the following issues:

The Needs of the Children. For example, a sickly or developmentally disabled child will often require a higher level of support than a healthy child.

The Age of the Children. Infants and younger children often cost less to support than older children.

The Ability of the Noncustodial Parent to Pay. The court is limited in awarding child support by the ability of a parent to pay based on income from all sources, often including a new spouse's earnings.

The Earning Capacity of the Custodial Parent. Both parents have the duty to support their children, not just the paying parent. Thus, the earnings or earning capacity of the custodial parent which are available to provide support for the children, and perhaps that of their new spouse, will also be considered when determining child support levels.

The Other Responsibilities of the Parents. The other lawful responsibilities of both parents will also be looked into in determining child support. For example, if the noncustodial parent is paying child support from a previous marriage (a rather common occurrence), the court will take that obligation into consideration. Necessities of life, such as rent and food will also be taken into account by the court. However, the court will not reduce child support payments to make it easier for the parent to pay discretionary obligations. For example, a parent cannot provide for a charity or buy an expensive car at the expense of providing for his or her own children. And if push comes to shove a parent will have to pay child support instead of MasterCard if he or she does not have the means to pay both.

To assist the court in determining the proper amount of support, both parties will be required by the court to prepare a financial declaration that is signed under penalty of perjury. (The court clerk will have the proper form to use.) Each parent will be required to fully disclose their income (from all sources, frequently including money earned by a new spouse or live-in lover), the nature and extent of their property holdings such as bank accounts, investments and real property and their financial obligations. The court will rely heavily on these documents in making the order, and thus it is in the best interests of the children that the declarations be filled out completely and honestly.

Child support hearings are often adversarial. That means that when the parents cannot agree on the support order (sometimes after mandatory mediation), the court will hold a hearing to decide the issue. (This is sometimes done in a chamber's conference to save time.) At the hearing or trial, each spouse (or their lawyer) will have the opportunity to cross-examine the other on issues relevant to the support issue and each can subpoena documents and call witnesses to support his or her position as to the amount of child support that should be paid. (If you choose to represent yourself, subpoena forms are available from the court clerk.) Child support orders can also be appealed, although the likelihood of success is very slim.

As can be seen from the above discussion, establishing child support payments can be a very subjective process. This has often led to uneven results with some judges ordering higher levels of support than others based on similar circumstances. For this reason and to ensure that child support payments are sufficiently high to keep children out of poverty (divorce is a primary cause of poverty among children), many courts have created rules which use complex formulas that judges are to follow when setting child support. Supporting parents often have to pay close to 50% of their net earnings in support, if they have more than one or two children.

Other Child Support Issues

There are other issues that parents need to understand regarding child support.

Only the Proper Court Has the Power to Order Child Support. A court that does not have proper *jurisdiction* (power) does not have the legal authority to order child support. In order for a court to have jurisdiction to compel a parent to pay child support, it must have *personal jurisdiction* over the parent. Personal jurisdiction means that the parent from whom support is sought must have sufficient contacts with the state in which the suit is brought. Thus, if a suit is brought for child support in South Dakota and the parent from whom support is sought has only been in that state once while on vacation at Mount Rushmore, the South Dakota court would not have personal jurisdiction and would not be able to award child support—even if the children and the custodial parent lived in the state.

A State that Entered a Valid Support Order Continues to Have the Power to Modify Child Support. Once a valid child support order is entered, that state continues to have the power to award child support even though it no longer has contacts with the supporting parent or children.

The following are examples of how these two principles work in real life:

> Christopher and Audrey and their children lived in Arizona. Audrey left Christopher and took the children with her to Michigan. One year later, she filed for divorce and sought custody and child support in Michigan. The court awarded Audrey custody and granted her divorce. However, it could not award child support because Christopher had no contacts with Michigan. Audrey was forced to seek a support order in Arizona.
>
> Charlie and Anne were divorced in Michigan. Charlie was awarded custody and Anne paid $300 a month in support. Anne moved to Arizona and never returned to Michigan. Five years later, Charlie sought an increase in child support in the Michigan court. Anne challenged the power of the Michigan courts to modify the order on the basis that it did not have personal jurisdiction over her because she no longer had contacts with that state. The court modified the order despite the fact that Anne did not have any contacts with Michigan, because its jurisdiction continued from the original decree.

Parents Can Agree on the Level of Support. Parents frequently settle divorce or paternity cases between themselves without going to trial, including issues of child support. Sometimes, this happens because of mediation or because their attorneys helped facilitate the agreement. These settlements are usually accepted by the court and take a lot less time and money to fashion. However, if the court believes the settlement has been coerced, or if the settlement is not deemed by the court to be in the best interests of the children, it does not have to accept the agreement as it relates to child support and can enter a different order.

Hugh and Lucy divorced. In a marital settlement agreement (see Chapter 7), they agreed that Lucy would have custody of the children. However, Hugh would only agree to pay $50 per month in child support, despite the fact he earned $2000 a month. Rather than fight Hugh, who had threatened a custody fight if she would not accept the deal, Lucy agreed to the low support level. When Lucy and Hugh brought their "agreement" before the court, the judge refused it because the support level was too low.

Courts Can Order Payment of College Expenses Even Though the Child Has Reached Majority. At one time, majority was reached at age 21. When it was reduced by law to age 18, a new problem was presented: Could a court order a parent to pay for his or her children's college expenses as child support, despite the fact that they would be over 18 when the payments were made? In most states, that question has been answered in the affirmative—if the parent has sufficient resources—although courts are not required to make such orders.

Child Support Is Not Tax-deductible. Unlike alimony, payments of child support cannot be deducted from the payer's income taxes. However, if your child stays in your home more than 50% of the time, you can claim the child as a dependent to save money on taxes. Parents often agree on the issue of the dependent's deduction so that both don't make the claim, which could trigger an I.R.S. audit.

MODIFYING CHILD SUPPORT

The court that makes the original child support award is said to have *continuing jurisdiction* to modify the order as conditions warrant. That being so, either parent may request the court to change the order throughout the duration of the child's minority. Modifications will not happen automatically. One of the parents must request the change by a formal motion to the court.

Child support orders cannot be changed on caprice or because a court thinks that "it is time." It must be based on evidence proving that sufficient grounds exist to make the change. This usually requires a showing of *changed circumstances* from the facts as they existed at the time that the last order was entered. (In the many years a child support order remains effective, the parent's circumstances may change many times and thus so may the child support order.)

Many different scenarios can create changed circumstances. For example, if the paying parent has had a large increase in income, the court can order the child support increased. Or, if the child's needs grow, such as when the child becomes ill or disabled, the amount of support can be ordered raised. Sometimes the mere passage of time creates the changed circumstances. For example, as a child grows older, it becomes more expensive to buy clothes, food and other necessities. These increased expenses can be enough to justify a raise in the support order.

Support can also be reduced upon a proper showing. For example, if the custodial parent inherits money, gets a large raise or otherwise has an increased ability to support the children, support payments may be reduced. Or, if the paying parent loses his or her job, the court can be asked to reduce support during the period of unemployment.

A mistake many parents make is to reach informal oral agreements modifying child support. This often provides the seed for future discord. For example, the following scenario is very common:

> Lyle paid his former wife Elaine $400 a month to support their son. When Lyle was laid off, he called Elaine and said, "I just got laid off. I can't afford to pay $400 right now." Elaine responded, "Okay. Pay $100 for now."
>
> Ten months later, Lyle was rehired and raised his support payments back to $400. During his layoff, Lyle had made 10 payments of $100. Elaine called and told Lyle she expected him to pay the $3,000 he had not paid during the layoff. Lyle replied that he did not owe the money because they had agreed to the child support reduction during his layoff. Elaine disagreed. She claimed that she had not given up the right to $400 a month but had merely permitted Lyle to defer full payment until he was rehired.
>
> When Lyle refused to pay, Elaine took him to court. The judge ruled that the evidence did not support Lyle's claim that he was excused from $300 per month of his support during his layoff and he was ordered to pay the $3,000 to Lyle at the rate of $100 a month, in addition to the usual payments of monthly support.

The problem with oral agreements is that they are often vaguely worded and the memories or understanding of the parties may often differ. Thus, any agreement by parents to modify child support should be put in writing so that there are no misunderstandings later on. It is also a good idea to have a judge sign a court order based on the agreement. (Your local library will have form books illustrating the proper forms of a stipulation and court order to modify child support.)

ENFORCING CHILD SUPPORT

A major headache for custodial parents, children and society is created when a parent refuses to pay his or her court ordered child support. This is a serious problem of national dimensions. A recent study found that less than half the parents awarded child support receive payment in full. In 1989 alone, *$4 billion* dollars that was owed in child support was not paid. This failure on the part of noncustodial parents—usually but not always fathers—is a major cause of poverty among children. This not only affects the families but has an indirect impact on society, which must finance poverty programs to assist those in need.

As a result of this problem, specific laws and systems have been created to help. Each state also has child support enforcement offices (see Appendix 2), usually run by state and local human service departments. Child support enforcement offices can help the custodial parent find an absent parent and collect chid support payments. The custodial parent has other tools available to enforce child support orders, all of which should be considered if payments are not being made:

Use the Government's Parent Locator Service

Nonpaying parents often hide from the custodial parent in order to avoid their child support obligation, often going so far as to move out-of-state to avoid their responsibilities. Such abandonments have caused many parents to go on welfare.

In order to remedy this problem, the federal government has created the *Parent Locator Service,* which allows the resources of the federal government, including the Social Security Administration and the Internal Revenue Service, to be used to locate a nonpaying parent's employer. Once found, the custodial parent or the state can enforce the child support order and collect unpaid support. The law also permits the I.R.S. to pay child support arrears from tax refunds the nonpaying parent may be owed by the government. (The law also requires the states to establish a Parent Locator Service.) For more information on the Parent Locator Service, contact your local office of the Department of Health and Human Services. (The telephone number will be in the government section of your telephone book under U.S. Government.)

Obtain a Wage Assignment

Many states allow the court to order an employer to make direct payments to the custodial parent from the wages of the supporting parent. This procedure is known as a wage assignment. The wage assignment can be issued upon proper application by the court and served on the paying parent's employer. Once implemented, the employer will deduct child support like any other deduction from the paying parent's paycheck and send the money directly to the custodial parent. This is a very valuable tool—if the nonpaying parent holds a steady job.

Request a Writ of Execution

A child support order can be enforced like other court judgments. If the nonpaying parent has assets such as real property, bank accounts, stock, a paid-off car or other property, the property may be seized upon proper application to the court.

If you choose to represent yourself, you will find form books in your local law library that will have the proper wording of the documents and will explain the procedure for applying for a contempt of court citation, wage assignment, or writ of execution in your state.

Bring a Civil Contempt of Court Action. If a person willfully disobeys a lawful child support order, he or she can be jailed for contempt of court. The civil contempt action is brought by the custodial parent. The court clerk will have the proper forms. After you file the proper forms, the nonpaying parent will have to be served with process, (that is, formally notified) since he or she has a constitutional right to appear at the hearing and present a defense. If the nonpaying parent is served with process and does not appear, the trial court will order a bench warrant issued for his or her arrest.

If the court finds beyond a reasonable doubt that the parent has willfully failed to pay pursuant to a valid child support order, the court can order the nonpaying parent jailed. (A parent who can show that they did not have the ability to pay will not be found in contempt of court, even though he or she will continue to owe the money.)

Often, the mere *threat* of jail is sufficient to pry open the recalcitrant parent's pocketbook. However, in severe cases, parents will be jailed and often the jail sentence will be open-ended, terminating only when the proper payment has been made.

Seek a Criminal Prosecution

All states also have criminal statutes on the books to punish parents who refuse to pay their child support. If the custodial parent complains to the district attorney's office, it may seek an indictment against the nonpaying parent in criminal court. If the defendant is found guilty, he or she may be jailed. Or, the guilty parent may be put on probation and allowed to remain free if he or she pays all back child support and makes all future payments in a timely manner.

In addition to the above, many custodial parents have questions about child support enforcement. Here are the answers to the most common:

I Want to Hire an Attorney to Help Me Enforce Child Support, But I Don't Have the Money. What Do I Do? Many states now require a court to order the nonpaying parent to pay the attorneys' fees and costs incurred in child support enforcement actions. Thus, ask the attorney you plan to hire whether he or she will defer the fee and obtain it from the nonpaying parent. Some attorneys will do this, or permit you to make monthly payments while pursuing the nonpaying parent. Others will require up-front payment in full and will reimburse you if the fees are subsequently paid by the nonpaying parent pursuant to court order.

How Long Do I Have to Enforce the Child Support Order? That will vary from state-to-state; usually, 10 years.

Can I Collect Interest on Unpaid Support? Yes, at the legal rate set by the law of your state (usually between 8–10%).

Is There Anything I Can Do to Enforce My Child Support If My Former Spouse Moves Out of State? In addition to the remedies mentioned above, the *Uniform Enforcement of Support Act* permits you to complain to your local district attorney about unpaid support. The office will then contact the district attorney in the locale where the nonpaying child supporter lives. That office, in turn, will bring an action to enforce the order on your behalf. (For more information, contact your local district attorney's office.) You can also register the child support order with the court in the state where the child support payor lives and then apply directly to that state for enforcement of the order.

My Ex-spouse Is Going Bankrupt and Owes Me $5,000 in Back Support. Am I Out of Luck? For the time being, maybe, but not in the long run. Child support orders are not dischargeable in bankruptcy. (In fact, if your ex gets out from under the crush of debts, he or she may be more likely to pay you. At the very least, you won't be competing with a hoard of other creditors for the few dollars that may be available.)

My Former Spouse Has Stopped Paying Support. I Don't Want to Hurt His Feelings By Going to Court. Am I Making a Mistake? Enforcement of child support orders are best done early rather than late. If there is good cause to reduce payments, an agreement can be made. However, if the parent is merely making excuses, taking immediate and tough action to enforce the court order will be most likely to convince the nonpaying parent that failure to pay will have serious consequences. Moreover, if the amount owed (*arrears*) gets too high, the nonpaying parent may never have the ability to pay it all back.

Parents who refuse to pay child support are merely the tip of the iceberg of a growing problem in the United States of family discord and breakdown. The nature of these problems and what can be done about them is the subject of our next chapter.

11

FAMILY
VIOLENCE

Today's families commonly face difficulties that were thought relatively rare just a few decades ago: spousal and child abuse are realities with which many families must cope. The manner in which the law seeks to cope with these severe family problems, primarily domestic violence and child abuse, is the focus of this chapter.

DOMESTIC VIOLENCE

Domestic violence is a problem of growing national concern. An estimated 4 million American women are battered each year by their husbands or partners and 50% of all American women are battered at some time in their lives. According to FBI statistics, approximately 95% of domestic violence victims are women and 5% are men. Research indicates that between 90% and 43% of the time, spousal abuse is not reported. For example, an April 1993 study conducted by the Family Violence Prevention Fund found that 14% of women report they have been the victim of beatings and other physical abuse by a husband or boyfriend. Indeed, medical research indicates that more women are seriously injured by beatings than by car accidents, muggings, and rape combined. In fact, FBI crime reports indicate that 30% of all female homicide victims each year are killed by their husbands and boyfriends.

People who abuse others have a strong need to exercise power and control over the lives of their victims. If exerting power and control by other means doesn't work, an abuser will turn to violence. The following are common behavioral patterns of batterers:

Using Intimidation. Making victims afraid by using looks, actions and gestures, smashing things, destroying property, abusing pets, or displaying weapons.

Using Emotional Abuse. Putting a battered woman down, making her feel bad about herself, calling her names, making her think she's crazy, playing mind games, convincing her that she is worthless, convincing her that no one would ever accept her word over his, humiliating her or making her feel guilty.

Using Isolation. Controlling what the battered woman does, who she sees and talks to, what she reads, where she goes, limiting her outside involvement, using jealousy to justify actions, controlling her ability to communicate with the outside world by preventing her from learning English, preventing her from communicating with the police or not allowing her to communicate with family members.

Minimizing, Denying and Blaming. Making light of the abuse and not taking the battered woman's concerns about it seriously, saying that the abuse did not happen, shifting responsibility for abusive behavior to her, saying that she caused it, telling her that his actions were not abuse because the police arrived and did not arrest him.

Using Children. Making the battered woman feel guilty about the children, using the children to relay messages, using visitation to harass her, threatening to take the children away, assuring her that if she complains to the police or the court he will win custody of the children and she will never see them again.

Using Male Privilege. Treating the battered woman like a servant, making all the big decisions, acting like the "master of the castle" or being the one to define men's and woman's roles.

Using Economic Abuse. Preventing the battered woman from getting or keeping a job, making her ask for money, giving her an allowance, taking her money, not letting her know about or have access to family income, controlling all information regarding family expenses, preparing tax forms and mortgage or rental documents and ordering her to sign without allowing her to read what she is signing, controlling all information about family expenses, refusing to pay child support or paying child support late.

Using Coercion and Threats. Making and/or carrying out threats to do something to hurt her; threatening to leave her, commit suicide, or report her to welfare, I.R.S. or immigration officials; making her drop criminal charges; making her withdraw civil protection order petitions; making her do illegal things.

The Cycle of Violence

According to Lenore E. Walker, author of *The Battered Woman*, incidents of physical or sexual abuse are immediately followed by periods of affectionate behavior and promises that the batterer will reform his behavior.

For many victims it will take numerous times around this cycle of violence before they begin to understand that the violence will not stop merely because the batterer promises it will. Like alcoholism and substance abuse, batterers usually do not cure themselves and the violence will not end until they recognize it is the batterer, not the victim, who has the problem and take ownership of the abuse. Once this occurs, either because the police have intervened and arrested the batterer or because he has sought assistance from a batterers' treatment program, some batterers can learn alternative appropriate techniques for addressing their anger and frustration.

GETTING HELP

If you are a victim of domestic abuse, there is help available. Many victims seek help from friends, shelters, courts, or the police.

Community Shelters. Community shelters have been established to protect survivors using both private and public funds to support the programs. These shelters provide temporary lodging, food and other assistance, in addition to the protection of a "safe house," the location of which is kept secret from the abuser. Most communities have hotlines to assist abused spouses and live-in partners.

Civil Protection Orders (CPO). CPOs, which are now available in all states, are a powerful tool that the legal system offers to help protect victims of domestic violence from continued abuse. In virtually all states, a domestic violence victim may receive a CPO injunction from the family courts whether or not a criminal case is also being pursued against the abuser. Civil protection order remedies typically include orders:

- Not to molest, assault threaten, harass or abuse the victim.
- To stay away from her home, person, workplace and family members.
- To have no contact with the victim.
- To order the batterer out of the family home.
- To award temporary custody of minor children to the abused party.
- To award child and/or spousal support.
- To exchange personal property and automobiles.
- To order batterers into counseling.
- To order police assistance to the victim in enforcing and carrying out the CPO.

Once the order has been issued, victims should present a copy of the order to the police station closest to the their home, their employer and their children's school. If the order is violated the victim should call the police immediately. In most states violation of a CPO is a crime, a misdemeanor, for which the batterer must be arrested.

The Police. Most states have laws which permit police to arrest the perpetrator of domestic violence, even if the victim does not wish to press charges. (Frequently women who have just suffered a severe beating will be traumatized, non-communicative, and may lack self confidence; they fear that having the abuser arrested will result in worse violence later. Research however has shown that for most batterers, arrest itself is an effective deterrent to future domestic violence incidents.)

Arrest breaks the cycle of violence. Unfortunately, outdated attitudes die hard. While some police will treat domestic abuse cases seriously and victims with dignity and respect, others do not take action, treat the victim with disrespect and allow her to return to a dangerous situation. If this happens to you, you should obtain the police officer's name, badge number and the telephone number of the police station. If the officer threatens to arrest you as well (as some will do to avoid doing their jobs appropriately) back off and do not antagonize the officer. Take action to protect yourself from continued abuse by seeking shelter with friends, family members or a battered women's shelter. Take pictures of your injuries and if possible, any damage in the house where the incident occurred.

As soon as it is safe to do so, call the police station where the officer who came to your house works and demand to be allowed to speak with the captain or district commander. It is very important that you speak to the highest ranking officer that you can. Explain what happened and that the police officer failed to arrest your batterer. Ask that the case be assigned to an officer who will obtain your information and seek a warrant for your batterer's arrest. When a police officer is particularly helpful and does a good job in assisting you, it is also advisable to obtain the officer's name and badge number so that you can contact the supervisor to commend him or her for a job well done. Praise can often be more effective in changing police behavior in domestic violence cases than complaints.

Work with the Courts. Once the criminal justice system is involved in the case the person who has been abused should cooperate in the criminal prosecution of the abuser, especially since a condition of probation or release from jail will be for the abuser to stay away from the victim. If your batterer has been ordered not to contact you, but he or his friends do, contact the prosecutor immediately so that the prosecutor can have his bail revoked and return him to jail until the trial has been completed. The criminal courts can, in addition to punishing the batterer with jail time:

- Order him into treatment.
- Require that he remain away from you.
- Require that he report for a period of years to a probation officer.
- Order that he pay compensation for medical bills and other expenses incurred as a result of the abuse.

File a Lawsuit. An abused person can also sue their spouse or partner for assault and battery in civil court. Assault and battery is a tort that if successfully proved, can result in a money judgment for items such as medical bills, lost wages and pain and suffering. It is an intentional tort and thus punitive damages may also be assessed to punish the wrong doer.

There is a tragic reality that must be mentioned. Doing everything listed above does not guarantee that an obsessed abuser will stay away from his victim, regardless of the legal consequences. The danger of domestic abuse increases rather than decreases directly after the parties' separation. In up to 75% of the domestic assaults reported to law enforcement agencies, the victim is already divorced or separated from the abuser at the time of the incident. In many cases, this danger continues for years after the parties have separated, particularly when the parties have children. For many seeking legal intervention from the police and the courts, however, the violence will stop.

In defending yourself during a domestic assault, it is important for victims to know that the law will only permit you to use the reasonable force necessary to defend yourself. Do not become the aggressor yourself or you may be subject to arrest.

PREPARE TO LEAVE

It is advisable that domestic violence victims prepare themselves so that they can leave when they decide it is safe. To be prepared to get away you should:

- Keep with someone you trust: a set of clothes, a spare set of keys, copies of important papers, prescriptions and some money.
- Keep any evidence of physical abuse in a safe place whether or not you have decided you wish to leave. Someday you may need this evidence. (Photos of injuries, bruises, destroyed furniture, ripped clothes, broken telephones.)
- Plan the safest time to get away.
- Know where you can go for help and tell someone what is happening to you. Have phone numbers of friends, relatives and domestic violence programs with you.
- Call the police if you are in danger and need help.
- If injured, go to the hospital emergency room or your doctor and report what happened to you and ask that they document your visit.
- Plan with your children and identify a safe place for them: a room with a lock or a neighbor's house where they can go for help. Reassure them that their job is to stay safe, not to protect you.
- Arrange a signal with a neighbor, e.g., if the porch light is on, call the police.
- Contact the local domestic violence hotline in your area to find out about local laws, the shelters and other resources available to you before you have to use them during a crisis.

Domestic violence is a serious social problem that the law alone may not completely remedy. The law can best help domestic violence victims who are willing to play an active role. It is best to protect yourself and your loved ones by knowing your rights and enforcing them vigorously through appropriate legal action. If you have further questions, contact your local domestic violence shelter or hotline or your local police department. If you have difficulty locating a local shelter program, contact the office of your local city council person who should be able to give you referral numbers or call the National Coalition Against Domestic Violence at (303) 839-1852.

CHILD ABUSE

One of the more disturbing phenomena of the past several decades has been the apparent growth in the level of parents and other adults who physically and sexually abuse children. (Some contend that the incidents haven't increased, merely the public awareness of them.) Not that child abuse never existed in history. It did. However, it is only since the 1950s that this country has recognized the depth of the problem.

The following 1992 statistics illustrate the depth and scope of the problem of child abuse in the United States:

- 2.9 million reports of child abuse were made.
- It is estimated that 45 out of every 1,000 children are abused.
- This was an increase in reports of child abuse of 50% over 1985 levels.
- There were 1,261 children who were killed due to child abuse in 1992.
- Of these, 85% were under the age of five.
- 43% of the children killed by abuse were under the age of one.

These are very disturbing statistics. What could cause adults to treat so many children so savagely? According to the experts, the causes are complex. However, certain factors have been identified as present in nearly all cases:

- The abuser was generally abused as a child.
- This caused the person to be unable to from a normal empathetic bond with his or her own children.
- The parent's expectations for the child is abnormally high and he or she lashes out at the child as punishment when those expectations are not fulfilled.
- Abuse is more likely to occur or may increase if the family is under significant stress.
- Drug and/or alcohol use by the abuser is common.
- If the child was the product of an unwanted pregnancy, that may aggravate the tendency toward abuse.

Child abuse is a problem that occurs in all regions, all socio-economic levels and among all ethnic, racial and religious groups in the country. No neighborhood is immune. The mistreatment of children also has legal and societal consequences beyond the immediate impact on the life of the abused. For example, child abuse is seen as a major factor in the growing crime problem this country faces, as many of the most violent felons in our penitentiaries suffered abuse as children.

The Definition of Child Abuse

The exact legal definition of child abuse varies somewhat from state-to-state, depending on the wording of each state's laws. Some states define child abuse in specific terms, listing wrongdoing such as bruising the child, causing him or her to experience bleeding, malnutrition, burns, broken bones, and soft tissue swelling. Also, sexual assault is listed, including fondling of private body parts and rape.

Child neglect, which is also considered abuse, is often defined as the failure to provide adequate nutrition, shelter, clothing or supervision for the child. Other states have laws which prohibit physical and sexual abuse and neglect generally, the exact definition to a case-by-case analysis. A few states now criminalize substance abuse by a pregnant woman as a form of child abuse because her baby may be born addicted, malnourished or developmentally disabled.

Child Abuse Reporting Laws

Child abuse often occurs in the privacy of homes and is therefore not witnessed directly by others. Often, the abuse is kept as a strict family secret never to be revealed to the outside world. In sexual abuse cases, the abuse may not even be known by anyone other than the abusing adult and the victimized child. Moreover, abused children are often too intimidated, afraid or ashamed to seek help. For these and other reasons, many cases of child abuse go unrecognized and/or unreported.

Under the law child abuse does not have to be directly witnessed to be reported. Indirect evidence of child abuse is often easier to spot: A teacher becomes concerned when a student often misses school and then returns bruised or injured. A doctor notices suspicious burns or other injuries during an examination or treatment. A child begins to "act out," wetting the bed or engaging in inappropriate sexualized behavior at a grandparent's home. Perhaps the abused child has confided to a friend about his plight and the friend alerts a minister, counselor or other trusted adult in authority. In fact, indirect evidence of child abuse often exists, waiting for a knowledgeable person to uncover it.

Under normal circumstances, there is no legal requirement that compels a citizen to report a crime. Thus, if a person sees a bank robbery in progress, he or she is not under a legal obligation to report it (although there is certainly a moral imperative). However, depending on who you are, the law is different when it comes to the crime of child abuse.

In order to better protect children and prevent abuse, the law *requires* professionals whose work involves children, such as teachers, doctors, social workers, psychiatrists and others, to report suspected cases of child abuse to the authorities. *Failure by these professionals to report suspected child abuse is a crime.*

These reporting laws create a powerful incentive to overcome the reluctance of some people to report child abuse because they "just don't want to get involved." (To ensure that these professionals do not turn a blind eye to the suspected abuse out of the understandable fear of being sued if their suspicions are mistaken, the law grants reporting professionals an immunity from being sued or prosecuted when they comply with reporting statutes. Such immunity statutes may not apply to average citizens.)

Court Action Against the Child Abuser

The authorities get involved in suspected child abuse cases when they receive a credible report that child abuse is suspected. Often, the complaint comes from a teacher or minister or other professional who has seen the evidence of child abuse and complies with the reporting statutes. Sometimes, it is reported by parents who have detected abuse in their own child or been told by the child that they were hurt. At other times, one parent reports the other parent, or a relative becomes suspicious and calls the police.

Initial Action to Protect the Child. When a report of child abuse is made to the authorities, swift action should happen.

(Unfortunately, what should happen doesn't always happen. Child welfare agencies are notoriously underfunded and understaffed. That means that some cases of reported abuse fall between the cracks. Thus, if you are making the report, act like the proverbial squeaky wheel and make sure the matter is aggressively pursued.)

Upon receiving the report, the social services department or other designated child abuse agency will begin an immediate investigation. If the investigator finds that the allegation is credible and if it is believed or it is obvious that the child is in need of protection, the child may be immediately removed from the home—if that is where the abuse occurred. (If the abuse seems to have occurred elsewhere, other action may be taken. For example, a day care center may be shut down if the authorities reasonably believe children are being abused at the facility.)

If the abuse is occurring in the home, a petition will be filed in juvenile court to bring the child under its jurisdiction and protection. (If the child is removed before court action is undertaken, the matter must be brought before a court's supervision without delay, usually within three days.)

Dependency Hearings. If authorities believe a child is being abused or neglected, they will bring an action in juvenile court. The purpose of the juvenile court hearing is to determine whether the parents should continue to have custody of the abused child or whether his or her custody should be transferred, at least temporarily, to the state.

At the hearing, the state will present evidence of the abuse or neglect. Witnesses will testify as to the facts that give rise to their belief that abuse or neglect occurred. For example, a physician may report on medical findings. A psychiatrist may testify that the child exhibits behavioral patterns consistent with having suffered abuse. A teacher may report that the child complained of beatings. Physical evidence, such as pictures of an injured child and medical records, may also be introduced. A child or parent may also testify to support the charge. (The courts go out of their way to make children feel as comfortable as possible in a difficult situation. For example, testimony may be given in the judge's chambers. Some courts permit testimony via closed-circuit television so that the child does not have to be in the same room as the alleged abuser.)

The accused parent also has the right to be heard. He or she can present the evidence from the same kinds of sources. The family doctor may testify that he or she has never seen any evidence to indicate abuse. The family minister may testify that the family has a good reputation in the church and that the children always seem happy and well adjusted. A psychiatrist hired by the accused may rebut testimony by the state's expert witnesses. The parent(s) may testify in their own behalf.

If it is found by the tough legal standard of *clear and convincing evidence* that the abuse occurred, the child is declared a dependent of the state, meaning his or her legal custody is now placed with the juvenile court. (This is not a criminal trial. Thus the more difficult to prove *beyond a reasonable doubt* evidentiary standard is not applied.) If the petition is denied, the parents retain custody.

Should the juvenile court sustain the charge, the abused or neglected child's legal custody will be transferred from the parents and the court will take control over the child's placement and care. In such cases, the court may decide to do one of the following:

Place the Child Back In the Home of the Parents. The courts will attempt to keep the family united if it can do so consistent with its legal duty to protect the welfare of the child. Accordingly, many dependent children are placed back into their own homes but under the court's supervision: This means that social workers and mental health professionals will monitor the family situation to ensure that the abuse has stopped. Also, the family will usually have to involve itself in treatment and therapy designed to teach members to interact in a nonabusive manner. The court's supervision will remain in effect until it is deemed to be unnecessary, at which point the custody of the child will be returned to the parents.

Place the Child With a Relative or Close Friend. If it is not in the best interests of the child to be returned to his or her parents' care, the court will try to find a temporary home for the child with someone the child already knows and trusts. Often, this is a grandparent, aunt or uncle, adult sibling, or close friend. While the child lives with the relative or friend, therapy will be mandated aimed at reuniting the family. (The court will offer referrals for therapy. Many of these facilities charge on a sliding scale.) Eventually, if family therapy is successful, the child may be returned to the parents under the supervision of the court to ensure that the family dysfunction has been remedied. If it has, the court will eventually dismiss the case and return legal custody to the parents.

Place the Child With Foster Parents. If a suitable relative or close friend is unavailable, the court may place the child in a foster home. Foster parents are people who agree to provide a temporary home for abused and other dependent children. Foster parents provide shelter, food and supervision for their foster children and are paid a stipend by the state for the cost of the care of their wards. While in foster care, the child and his or her family will receive treatment and therapy aimed at reuniting the family.

Keep Custody of the Child. As a last resort, the state may keep custody of the child in an institutional child care facility.

Here are a few examples based on real life cases:

Ray and Diana were having severe financial problems because Ray had been laid off at work. This placed them under extreme emotional stress as they were worried about losing their home. Ray already had a drinking problem and the layoff made his drinking worse.

Ray's depression grew worse and over several months he began to take his problems out on his eight-year-old son, James. It started with yelling and soon accelerated to slaps in the face. Diana was worried and upset but other than urging her husband to leave their son alone, she took no action to protect the boy. Then, one day, James, broke a window with a baseball. Ray, who was drunk at the time, became enraged. He grabbed James, knocked him down and then yanked him up by has arm so hard it broke the boy's arm. When James cried out in pain, Ray and Diana could see that the boy's arm was broken. They rushed the boy to the hospital.

Ray and Diana told the doctor in the emergency room that James had fallen out of a tree. But she saw old and new bruises on James' body. When asked how he broke his arm, James refused to answer. Believing the boy was a victim of abuse, the doctor immediately contacted her supervisor, who called the police pursuant to the state's reporting statute. The child protective service worker arrived and interviewed the child and parents, who broke down and told the truth. To be safe, she removed the child to a foster home pending a hearing.

(Continued)

Ray was truly remorseful. He cooperated fully with the juvenile court and accepted their taking legal custody of James. He promised to participate in family therapy and to go to Alcoholics Anonymous. The court decided to place the boy back into his parent's home, which was visited regularly by a social worker.

Two years later, Ray was not drinking and was back at work. The family was interacting better than it ever had and the juvenile court determined there was little risk that the abuse would be repeated. Accordingly, the case was dismissed and legal custody of James was returned to his parents.

Patricia was divorced, with a daughter named Wendy. Patricia married Hal when Wendy was 12. Patricia worked at night. About once a week, Hal would come into Wendy's bedroom to fondle her and engage in other sexual conduct. To keep Wendy quiet, he threatened to kill her puppy and her mother if she ever told anyone what he did to her. Wendy was terrified and kept quiet.

When Wendy was 14, she she told her mother what was going on. Her mother slapped her in the face and told her to quit lying about her husband. That night, Wendy attempted suicide and was later admitted into a psychiatric hospital. One day her biological father was visiting and Wendy became hysterical, screaming that her stepfather had raped her.

The hospital contacted the authorities. A petition was filed in juvenile court. Wendy was placed in the home of her father, who lived in another state. Wendy's stepfather was arrested and charged with child molestation. Wendy's mother remained hateful toward her daughter and was prohibited from seeing her without another adult to monitor the visits. No therapy was attempted because the bond between mother and daughter was broken.

Wendy's biological father filed for custody. Once it was granted, the juvenile court dismissed the case because it was convinced that Wendy's father could provide a proper home and provide his daughter with therapy to assist her in overcoming the effects of the abuse.

Although the nation's child dependency systems are underfunded and understaffed, they provide the only meaningful protection for abused and neglected children. Any one who reasonably believes that a child is being abused should be sure to report it.

If you ever find yourself in the juvenile court system, and if the allegations are true, be sure and cooperate with the court and social welfare department. Abusing parents who recognize their problems and who are willing to work to overcome them can expect the juvenile court experience to be a valuable, if difficult, experience. However, parents who stonewall and who resist assistance, or who have acted in a particularly brutal manner toward their children, may find that they lose their children altogether. These parents may also find that in addition to the civil actions taken by the juvenile court, that they face criminal prosecution.

Criminal Prosecution. Separate and apart from the proceedings in juvenile court, the district attorney can prosecute the abusing parent for child abuse or neglect in criminal court. If convicted, a child abuser may be imprisoned, ordered to keep away from the child, fined and/or ordered to undertake therapy or treatment. People convicted of sexual abuse will also have to register with the local law enforcement agency as a sex offender, wherever they may live.

The abuser is not the only one who may face criminal prosecution. It is not unusual for one parent to know that the other parent (or step-parent) is abusing their child. But rather than confront the abuser or report the abuser to the authorities, the parent keeps quiet, perhaps out of fear of losing a marriage, because they are abused themselves or they don't want to see their spouse hauled off to jail and thereby lose their sole means of support. But be aware: *It is a crime for a parent to allow a child to be abused even if the parent does not actively participate in the abuse.* Moreover, failing to protect a child could also result in the child being removed from the home altogether when the abuse is finally discovered. Thus, the lesson is clear: If a parent knows their child is being abused, the abuser should be reported immediately, if not only for the child's sake but for the sake of the nonabusing parent.

Guardianship Actions. Relatives such as grandparents, uncles and aunts or adult siblings of an abused or neglected child may wish to bring an independent action to obtain guardianship of the abused child. (A divorced parent can, of course, seek a change of custody in divorce court. See Chapter 9.) This action will take place in a probate or domestic law court, which can issue an order transferring custody from parent to guardian in appropriate cases. This can be a difficult goal to achieve, especially in marginal cases of neglect. The reason: There is a strong presumption in favor of retaining custody of children with parents. (In the event there is a conflict between the juvenile court order and the guardianship order, the juvenile court order predominates so long as it retains jurisdiction over the child.)

Child abuse is a serious problem that should concern everyone. If you have questions about the subject or suspect that a child you know is being abused, contact your community's child abuse reporting telephone number which you can find in the city/county telephone listings in your white pages telephone book. (Look for child abuse reporting lines under the "health department," "mental health," or "department of social services" listings.)

PART 4

OTHER
FAMILY ISSUES

12

MAKING
A HOME

The laws governing real estate transactions and rental agreements vary not only from state to state but in some instances, within a state, from one locality to the next. This chapter will describe, in general terms, what your legal rights are when you are buying or renting a home.

BUYING A HOME

Buying a home is usually the biggest financial transaction most people ever get involved in. No wonder many people approach a home purchase with fear and trepidation. A lot of money and emotional investment is at stake. However, when you are armed with knowledge, the fear should recede and be replaced with confidence—and the excitement of making a dream a reality.

The Real Estate Broker

Real estate *brokers* assist people in purchasing a home. Real estate brokers are professionals licensed by the state after obtaining sufficient education and passing a proficiency test. (Real estate *agents* are also tested and licensed. However, agents must work under the supervision of a broker.)

Real estate brokers and agents are permitted by law to work with both the seller and the buyer in the same sales transaction. This is a conflict of interest permitted by law. (A lawyer would not be able to work with both the buyer and seller in a financial transaction.)

Many buyers seek the assistance of a broker to help them find a house to buy; to give advice on the fair market price, financing tips and other important aspects of the hoped-for purchase; and to negotiate the terms of the sale. That is all well and good, but buyers should be aware that "their" agent may not actually represent them. Depending on the law of the state where the transaction occurs, the *selling agent* (the agent for the buyer who "sells" the property by bringing in the buyer) *may actually represent the seller.* That is because the selling and the *listing agent* (the agent for the seller who "lists" the property) split one commission that is paid for by the seller.

This means that when a listing agent brings you, the buyer, into a real estate deal, he or she may legally be a sub-agent of the listing agent. That also means that the *fiduciary* relationship (the duty of loyalty, trust and fair dealing) is owed to the seller and not to you! You should discuss this issue thoroughly with the agent before revealing any information you don't want disclosed to the seller.

Many states, recognizing the problem presented, have passed laws which permit the selling agent to work exclusively for the buyer, even though his or her compensation will be paid by the seller when the sale is complete. In such cases, the buyer, and not the seller, is owed the fiduciary duty and the purchase is more likely to be "at arms length." Thus, before working with the agent, ask him or her to "disclose" whether their fiduciary legal obligation is to you or the seller, and be sure the disclosures are in writing.

Sometime a listing agent may also represent the buyer. In such cases, buyers should be careful about disclosing their negotiating strategy since the agent may be duty-bound to tell the seller what was said. (For example, if the buyer tells the agent he wants to make an offer of $75,000 but will go as high as $85,000, the agent may be legally bound to disclose that information to the seller.)

Making an Offer

Once you find property you wish to buy, your next step (outside of searching for a loan) is to make an offer. The offer should be in writing. (If a real estate agent is being used, the agent will have the form and will "write up" the document. If there is no agent, the proper forms can be found in a stationery store.)

The offer should specify the following terms:

The Price That Is Offered. This can be lower, the same amount or higher than the listing price.

The Amount of Your "Earnest Money" Deposit. Your written offer should state that you are prepared to back up your offer with cash – called "earnest money." This is money you are ready to hand over as soon as your offer is accepted. Its purpose is to demonstrate your seriousness. It is not the down payment. Even on a very large, expensive house, $1,000-$5,000 in earnest money is quite routine. Whether your earnest money is refundable if the deal falls through is a matter for negotiation.

Who Pays the Costs of Sale. Every real estate deal has costs involved, such as *closing* fees and termite inspections. Your offer should state which party is responsible for such costs.

Contingency Clauses. It is very important for your offer to include contingency clauses that will let you cancel (*rescind*) the real estate contract (also known as the purchase agreement) under specified conditions. For example, you should always make the contract contingent upon obtaining financing so that the seller can't sue in the event your contract does not go through because you could not obtain a loan. The contract should also be contingent upon the seller having clear *title*. (The official record of ownership.)

Often, home defects, such as wiring or plumbing problems, will not be evident to the naked eye. Thus, another important contingency clause that should be placed in the offer is the right for you to pay for a professional home inspection and the unlimited right to cancel the contract if you're not satisfied with the result of the property report that will be made by the inspector.

Items to Be Included in the Sale

To prevent controversies over what is included in the purchase that could delay or even scuttle the sale, the offer should make sure to specify the items that you wish to have included in the purchase price. (Window treatments and appliances are often mentioned in such clauses.) *Fixtures*, items attached to the property, are automatically included as part of the sale unless the contract specifies otherwise. However, it is a good idea to list any unusual fixture that you wish to remain with the house in the offer. (For example, if there is an antique chandelier in the dining room or custom bookcases in the den, it is a good idea to specify in the offer that they are to be included in the sale.)

The offer should also require the seller to disclose in writing any known defects in the house or neighborhood. For example, structural problems, environmental hazards such as the presence of asbestos or radon gas, and neighborhood problems such as high crime or a planned freeway through the area should be required to be disclosed. In that way, you have an accurate idea of what is being purchased. Also, if material defects are hidden by the seller, he or she, and perhaps the real estate agent, can be sued for fraud.

An offer, if accepted, provides the terms of the contract of sale and will be legally binding. Thus, think through the offer carefully before communicating it to the seller.

The Counter Offer

At this point, the seller will usually counter offer. Legally, a counter offer is a rejection of the original offer and a new offer made by the seller to you, the potential buyer. A counter offer will often accept some terms of the offer and request changes in others. For example, an offer to buy the house for $75,000 might be "countered" with an offer to sell for $80,000. Once the counter offer is received it should be reviewed carefully to determine how the terms of the original offer were changed and to determine if new terms have been added that might be objectionable.

The Final Contract of Sale

Counter offers will often go back and forth until the parties either agree on all terms or break off negotiations. If the parties agree, the last counter offer will be signed by both parties and the contract will have been entered into.

A final real estate contract is generally assumed to be all-inclusive. Everything of importance should be written into it. Your contract should include the purchase price, down payment, a description of the property and a list of other items being sold with the house. It should specify how the ownership is to be transferred to you, the method of payment, the amount of the deposit, the conditions under which you or the seller can void the contract, any defects in the property or title, the settlement date and how financing will be arranged. Once signed, the contract is enforceable in court by either party according to the terms contained in the contract. If the parties do not come to an agreement on the terms, both are free to walk away from the negotiations without any obligation to the other whatsoever.

If your contract has provisions you don't understand, ask someone, possibly a lawyer, to interpret it. However, you probably don't need a lawyer to look after your interests, especially if you're already represented by a "buyer's broker" or have been through the process before.

Closing the Deal

When you have struck a deal with a seller and found your financing, it's time to pay for the property and receive the *deed* (the legal paper that proves you own the property). There's no standard name for this step. Depending on where you live, it may be called the *closing, title closing, settlement,* or *escrow.*

Often the closing takes place at a meeting of all those involved. When that happens, the process is commonly called a *settlement.* If no meeting occurs, it's more often known as *escrow* and is handled by an escrow agent. In such cases, you and the seller usually sign an agreement to deposit certain funds and documents with the escrow company, which acts as agent for both sides. When all the papers and funds are in, the escrow is closed and the agent records the documents and makes the appropriate payments.

Settlement, however, involves much more than the formal acts of passing the papers. All the details, loose ends and additional services required to conclude the deal must be tended to. This is when the full cost of buying a home becomes clear—not just the purchase price or the cost of the loan to buy it, but the actual costs of the process of buying as well. Be warned: these closing cost can add up to 8% of the purchase price of the home. As the buyer, you can expect to pay 3% to 6% of this purchase price sum.

FINANCING

Most home purchases must be made with the assistance of mortgage or trust deed financing. The following are some of the most important things to know about mortgage financing:

Types of Mortgages. Mortgages come in two basic types: fixed rate and variable rate. A fixed rate mortgage keeps the same interest rate for the life of the loan, typically 30 years. This also means the monthly payment remains unchanged for the life of the mortgage.

A variable rate mortgage starts at a lower interest rate than a fixed rate mortgage. However, the interest charged on the loan will vary every year, the amount usually depending on the fluctuations of an identified major economic index. This means that the mortgage payment will go up or down, depending on economic conditions. (If applying for a variable rate mortgage, be sure there is a cap above which the interest rate cannot go. Also, be sure there is a limit to the amount that the interest charged can be raised each year.) It is usually easier to qualify for a variable rate mortgage; however, over the life of the loan, a variable rate mortgage is likely to be more expensive.

The Down Payment. In order to get a loan, the mortgage lender will usually require you to put money down, typically

20%. With the price of real estate being what it is in many locales, this can be a problem, since a $300,000 property would require a down payment of $60,000 cash.

Some lenders will permit a lower down payment, even as low as 5%, if you obtain purchase mortgage insurance (PMI) to protect the lender against default. The price of the PMI will generally be based on a percentage of the purchase price, typically ½ of 1% up-front and about ⅓ of 1% per year after that. (Thus, on a $200,000 mortgage, the up-front PMI premium would be $1,000. Thereafter, the price would be about $666 per year, or a little more than $50 per month.) The PMI company has a lot of money at stake in the deal, and it will be very careful to ensure that the property is in good shape and that you are unlikely to default on the loan before agreeing to issue the insurance. Many home purchases have fallen through even though a bank has agreed to fund a mortgage when the PMI company refused to insure the loan.

Points. Most mortgage lenders charge points at the front end of the loan. A point is 1% of the loan. Thus a $100,000 mortgage financed at 2 points would cost $2000. (The points are usually paid through the loan; in the example above, the loan would actually fund at $102,000.)

Foreclosure. If the borrower defaults on the loan, the mortgage holder has the right to foreclose on the property; that is, have the property seized and sold at public auction to pay the unpaid balance on the loan.

Usually, foreclosure is the lender's only remedy if the loan goes into default. However, if the loan is not a purchase money mortgage (for example, if it is a refinancing to pay off debts), the lender may be able to foreclose and then seek money from the borrower for any unpaid balance. Before taking out a nonpurchase money mortgage, be sure to ask about the lender's remedies in the event of a default.

OWNING A HOME

The old saying, "a man's home is his castle" is not exactly true. Whatever was true when men owned castles, today's property owners do not have unlimited discretion as to how they use their property. Here are some of the legal limitations that exist in most communities.

Obligations of the Property Owner

Property owners have obligations to their community and neighborhood that can be enforced in a court of law. Briefly, these obligations include:

Paying Property Taxes. Property taxes must be paid, or the municipality can seize the property and sell it at auction to pay back taxes. The amount of tax is usually based on a percentage of the appraised value of the property.

Meeting Local Codes. If a homeowner wants to improve the property, he or she will have to comply with local building codes. The use of the property (e.g. residential, commercial, etc.) will be limited by local zoning regulations.

Maintaining the Property. Municipalities can use civil and criminal laws to prevent property owners from permitting their property from falling into disrepair and from allowing the property to become a public hazard. Failure to maintain the property can also result in a civil suit brought against the owner by neighbors.

Complying With Home Owners' Association Rules. Some neighborhoods have home owners' associations, which set rules on the upkeep of the homes under their jurisdictions. Home owners' associations can set standards of upkeep, paint color, home improvements, building heights and other such matters that would normally be exclusively under the property owner's control.

Condominium Ownership

Owners of condominiums and townhomes have special rules which apply.

Each Owner Owns His or Her Own Unit and a Proportionate Share of the Common Areas. Thus, each is responsible for the costs of maintaining their individual unit and for maintaining and repairing common areas, such as swimming pools, walkways, roofs and walls, in direct proportion to their ownership interest. (If there are 50 units in a condominium complex, an owner would be responsible for 1/50 of the common area maintenance and repair costs.) These expenses are paid for by the condominium association, financed through dues paid by each owner.

Each Owner Must Join the Condominium Association. The management decisions for the condominium complex will be made by the condominium association, usually through its board of directors, elected by the association members. Often, managers will be hired by the board to manage the day-to-day affairs and maintenance of the complex.

Each Owner Must Pay Association Dues. To make sure that the complex is maintained, each owner pays dues to the association. The dues pay for maintenance, normal repair, insurance, the complex manager's salary and other such expenses. The amount of the dues will be established by the board, usually in an amount sufficient to maintain and repair the premises and to create a fund for emergencies. Failure to pay dues can result in a lawsuit and/or a *lien* (a legal claim) being placed on the owner's condominium property.

The Association Can Levy a Special Assessment to Improve or Repair the Property. In an emergency, a special assessment can be charged by the association to repair the complex. For example, if there is a mudslide that damages the property, the owners can be assessed the money it will take to repair the damage, even if the individual owner's unit is not actually damaged.

The Association Sets the Rules for the Complex. The condominium association sets rules that all residents of the condominium complex must obey. These rules may range from prohibiting owners from parking their cars in their driveways, to requiring association permission before improving a unit, to a prohibition from playing the stereo too loud, to permitting cats but not dogs to be kept in the complex. Failure to obey the rules can result in fines being assessed by the association or other enforcement actions.

SELLING A HOME

Selling a home is the other side of the coin to buying a home, and the discussion above regarding offer, counter offer and closing apply. However, there are differences between buying and selling that need to be discussed:

The Listing Agreement

Most sellers use real estate brokers to sell their property. This is done by contract, usually known as a *listing agreement*. The listing agreement will:

Establish the Broker's Compensation. Real estate brokers and agents are paid a percentage of the selling price. They will usually ask for 6%. However, feel free to negotiate the amount. Many will accept 5% or even less, depending on market conditions.

Set the Time the Agreement Will Be in Effect. The listing agreement will be in effect for the amount of time established in the contract, usually six months. During that time, the seller can cancel the listing. However, if the agreement is cancelled, the seller will not be able to select another company to list the property until the original contract period has lapsed.

Probably Be an Exclusive Listing. Technically, a seller can arrange for many brokers to represent the property. However, in real life, most real estate brokers will insist on an "exclusive listing." If that is the agreement, no other real estate company can be given a listing during the time the first agreement is in effect.

DEALING WITH THE BROKER

The Broker May Be Entitled to a Commission

The listing broker's job is to find a qualified buyer to purchase the seller's property at the terms set forth in the listing. If such a buyer is found, who makes an offer to meet all of the material terms of the listing, or if a deal is made and subsequently the seller gets cold feet, the broker may still be owed a commission. (If the offer is for less than the listed terms, no commission would be owed. Also, if the deal falls through at the closing or settlement stage because a failure of a contingency or the buyer backs out, the seller would not owe a commission.)

The Broker's Responsibilities

The broker's responsibilities will be set forth in the written listing agreement. The responsibilities should include advertising the property at the broker's expense, listing the property on the multiple listing service, holding open houses, etc. The broker should also give expert advice on the listing price, terms and negotiating strategy. The seller should be sure that the broker's obligations are set forth in the agreement.

The Duty to Disclose

Increasingly, state laws are being passed requiring detailed disclosure by sellers about facts and conditions that they know would materially effect the buyer's decision to purchase. Failure to disclose such conditions can give rise to liability for fraud once the true conditions become known. Thus, if there has been a flood in the area, it should be disclosed. If the roof leaks or the plumbing needs repair, it should be disclosed. If the house has had structural problems, advise the buyer. All disclosures should be in writing, signed by the buyer and seller, so that the seller can prove that the necessary disclosures were made.

A Purchase Agreement Is Enforceable in Court

A contract for the purchase of real property is enforceable in court. However, it *must be in writing*. Otherwise, it violates the *statute of frauds* (laws in each state that specify which contracts must be in writing to be considered legal and enforceable).

Enforcement can include the following remedies:

Specific Performance. A seller can obtain a court order compelling the buyer to go through with the deal under the terms of the contract. This works both ways if the seller is the one who has second thoughts.

Money Damages. Often, when a deal falls through, it is because the buyer does not have the money to complete the deal or the buyer changes his or her mind. In such cases, a seller may elect to sell the property to someone else. If the price is less than the original contract, the first prospective buyer can be made to pay the difference. Sellers (and buyers) can also sue for out-of-pocket losses, such as fair rental value when the property was "off the market," or other damages that were caused because the deal did not go through.

RENTERS AND THE LAW

Not everyone owns their own property. Millions of people happily rent their homes. The first major contract many of us sign is to rent a house or apartment. Yet, most of us don't read our leases carefully beyond checking the amount of monthly rent and the length of the lease. It's important for renters to understand their rights and obligations. This section provides some general answers. More information on local rental laws may be available through tenants' rights associations which, in larger urban areas, often operate telephone "hotlines" that offer free advice.

The Rental Agreement

Rental agreements control the rights and obligations of the owner of the property, called the landlord, and the renter, called the tenant. The agreement will usually be in writing but it does not have to be. The terms in the agreement generally include the following:

Time. Rental agreements are either based on a lease or are month-to-month. A lease gives the tenant the right to live in the premises for a specific period of time, for example, one year, even if the property is sold. During that time, if the tenant complies with the contract, he or she cannot be forced to leave, and the rent cannot be raised.

If the tenant vacates the property before the end of the lease, he or she can be held liable for the unpaid rent to the end of the lease period. In such cases, the landlord has the obligation to try and mitigate (reduce) the renter's damages by finding another tenant. Failure by a landlord to attempt to mitigate damages can reduce the amount of damages the landlord will receive in court.

Charlie leased a house for one year for the price of $1,000 a month. Four months later, he was transferred to another town. He asked to be let out of the lease, but the landlord refused. Charlie moved with six months remaining on the lease, giving the landlord written notice that he had vacated the premises.

The landlord did not try to rent out the property but demanded that Charlie pay the $6,000 in unpaid rent. Charlie refused, and the landlord kept the property vacant because he wanted to collect the money from Charlie.

The two went to court. Charlie proved that houses such as the landlord's could be expected to rent out within 30 days of being on the market. The court concluded that the landlord would only have lost one month in rent if he had attempted to mitigate Charlie's damages. Thus, Charlie was only ordered to pay the landlord $1,000 for breaching the lease instead of $6,000.

Leases usually have terms that apply at the end of the lease period. For example, if the lease is not canceled in writing, it may automatically renew. Or, it may cease to be a lease, but continue on a month-to-month basis. It is important to understand such clauses so that there are no unpleasant legal surprises when the tenancy expires.

A month-to-month agreement, as the name applies, continues in effect one month at a time. During the month, the tenant's rent cannot be raised and the tenant cannot be evicted. But, rent increases (absent rent control) and eviction can occur upon 30 days' written notice. Conversely, a renter may terminate the lease within 30 days' written notice.

The Amount of Rent. The rental agreement or lease will establish the monthly rent to be paid and the date the rent is due. It will also contain a penalty amount for rent that is paid late.

The Rules of the Premises. The rental agreement will also require the tenant to maintain the premises, and may contain rules against such things as nailing pictures to the wall, keeping pets and allowing others to live on premises without the landlord's consent.

Miscellaneous Terms. The agreement will also probably contain clauses permitting the landlord to collect his or her attorneys' fees incurred in enforcing the agreement. (Such clauses give the tenant reciprocal rights, even if that is not stated in the contract.) Other terms may include identifying the address where notices are to be sent and provisions relating to the payment of security, key and cleaning deposits.

The Right to a Habitable Home

Renters have legal rights that may not appear in the rental agreement. First and foremost among these is the right to have the landlord maintain the property so that it remains habitable. Thus, if the landlord does not provide running water, electricity or pest control, action can be taken to force the landlord to do so. Such action may include withholding rent, the tenant doing the work and forcing the landlord to reimburse him or her for such expenditures, and criminal prosecution. (Some "slumlords" have been sentenced in such cases to living in their own buildings.)

Tenants should be sure they understand the law before they take any action against landlords who do not provide a habitable premise. Legal clinics often handle such cases or provide counseling on renter's rights.

Rent Control

Many cities have rent control laws that restrict the ability of landlords to raise rent. Usually, such laws provide that rent cannot be raised above a specified percent per year, with exceptions for allowing landlords to recap expenses incurred in improving the property. Often, these laws do not apply to apartments once they are vacated. That can create a powerful financial incentive to make life tough on a long-term tenant who is paying lower than the current market value in rent. Thus, tenants in rent-controlled cities may have to be aggressive in enforcing their rights to live in a habitable apartment and to having their apartment maintained adequately pursuant to the rental agreement.

Unlawful Detainer

If a renter falls behind on the rent or violates the lease or rental agreement in some material manner, the landlord may begin eviction proceedings. This is usually accomplished in a lawsuit called *unlawful detainer*. An unlawful detainer case can result in the sheriff physically evicting the tenant. Also, a tenant who is found to have willfully refused to vacate for failing to pay rent may be ordered to pay punitive damages, usually three times the amount of unpaid rent.

Renters sometimes have a defense to an unlawful detainer case, known as retaliatory eviction. If the renter can prove that the eviction is not about past due rent or the violation of the rental agreement but is actually brought because the tenant enforced his or her renter's rights, the renter may be able to win the eviction case. Here is an example based on a real case:

> Margaret's landlord refused to maintain her apartment building. The neglect became so bad that the landlord was in violation of city laws. Margaret grew tired of continually fighting with the landlord about the condition of the property. So, she called the housing authority when the landlord refused to repair water damage to the interior of her apartment and fumigate the building to eradicate a cockroach infestation.
>
> Shortly thereafter, the landlord served Margaret with an eviction notice claiming that the unit was being taken off the market so that the landlord's sister could live there. Margaret defended the eviction, claiming the move was retaliatory for her turning the landlord in to the authorities and was really aimed at freeing an apartment that could be rented for $100 more per month to a new tenant. Margaret won her case and the eviction was refused by the court.

Fighting a wrongful eviction can be emotionally draining and time-consuming. Moreover, it may require hiring an attorney who knows the details of eviction law. Luckily, in many locales there are legal clinics to assist people with landlord/tenant problems, especially people who have a low income. Some law schools also provide assistance to people in a clinic setting.

13

BUYING INSURANCE

Insurance is a huge business. In the United States alone there are approximately 5,800 insurance companies that generate premiums of over $600 billion for all types of insurance. According to the National Insurance Consumer Organization, the average American family spends almost $3,000 every year in out-of-pocket premiums and about $4,500 in indirect payments (insurance paid by employers or by businesses with the cost passed through to consumers in the price of goods). This amounts to approximately 12% of the disposable income in the United States. In fact, Americans pay more for insurance than they do for federal income taxes, not counting Social Security.

People also benefit from the insurance they purchase. Homeowners rely on insurance to rebuild their homes if a fire destroys it. Drivers rely on insurance to protect their assets in the event of an accident. It is difficult to obtain quality medical care without health insurance.

This chapter will address legal issues of insurance, including life, health, auto and homeowner's. Among the topics addressed will be: the anatomy of an insurance policy, the difference between term and cash value life insurance policies, the law that permits laid-off workers and divorcing spouses to keep employer-provided health insurance, and the methods policyholders can use to enforce their rights.

THE ANATOMY OF AN INSURANCE POLICY

An insurance policy is, in reality, a contract. Under the contract, the policyholder pays premiums to the insurance company; in return, the company promises to pay for losses suffered by the policyholder that are identified in the insurance contract. That seems simple, but as some say, the devil is in the details.

The details are found in the insurance policy itself. Too many people don't read their own insurance policies and many insurance agents do an inadequate job of fully explaining the terms and conditions of coverage. As a result, insurance buyers may not always know what hazards they are protected against, and, perhaps more importantly, what hazards are not covered by the policy. The following are questions each policyholder must answer if he or she is to know his or her rights vis-a-vis their insurance company.

What Is Covered?

To find out what is covered in an insurance policy, look at the *endorsements* section of the policy. There you will find the following information:

- The name and address of the insurance company.
- The type of policy.
- The name and address of the insured.
- The exact time the policy is in effect.
- The extent of coverage.

For example, an auto insurance policy might provide that the policy is in effect from 12:01 A.M. on March 1, 1994, until midnight February 28, 1995. If an accident that would be covered by the insurance policy happens during that time, the insurance company must pay benefits. However, if it happens even minutes outside the time that is covered, the company will probably have no obligation. The endorsements page is a summary of the policy. For example, the endorsements page in an auto policy will describe the amount of coverage, the deductibles (what the policyholder must pay before the company has to pay) and any additional coverage that has been purchased (called a rider or an endorsement, depending on the type of policy) not already covered under the basic insurance policy.

The exact terms of the coverage will be found later in the agreement section. Be sure to read the agreement section in addition to the declarations page in order to understand the exact nature of the insurance coverage.

What Isn't Covered?

Every policy will restrict the scope of coverage in the policy by removing areas of risk that would otherwise come under the insurance umbrella. These are known as *exclusions.* For example, a homeowner's policy that covers the policyholder against damages caused by his or her own negligence, will exclude from protection any damages caused while driving a car. (Thus, a homeowner will need both homeowner's insurance and auto insurance.)

How Do I Know What the Words in the Policy Mean?

To make sure that the company and policyholder understand the meaning of specific terms used in the insurance contract, there is a definitions section in every policy. For example, assume a policy states that it protects "you from liability for damages caused to others by your negligence." Assume further that the policyholder lives with a domestic partner but is not married. Then assume that the policy contains the following typical policy definition:

Throughout this policy, "you" and "your" refers to: 1. The named insured on the declarations page, and 2., the spouse if a resident of the same household.

Under this policy, the domestic partner would *not* be covered under the policy because of the way the words "you" and "your" are defined in the policy as including only the named policyholder and a spouse living in the same household. Since a domestic partner is not a spouse, extra coverage might have to be purchased to protect the domestic partner, even though he or she lives with the policyholder.

How Do I Make a Claim?

The manner in which a claim is filed with the company will also be set forth in the policy. This too must be read and understood, because failure to comply with the proper procedure could delay payment.

THE CLAIMS PROCESS

When an insured person suffers a loss covered by insurance, a claim must be made to the company in order to receive benefits. The method by which that is done will be specified in the policy. It's important to note that it is not always necessary to hire an attorney to file a claim, either with your own insurer or with the insurer of someone who has injured you. In fact, there is ample evidence that attorney involvement drives up the total cost of settlement without increasing the net benefit to claimants. Whether or not you will need attorney assistance will depend on how comfortable you are negotiating directly with the insurer.

Generally, here's how the claims process works:

- The claim is filed.
- It is sent to an adjuster, usually but not always an employee of the insurance company, who will investigate the claim.
- Once the claim is investigated, the company will either reject the claim, or offer to pay the claim.
- If the claim is rejected and the policyholder believes the rejection was in error, he or she will have to take steps to enforce the policy provisions (see below). If the claim is accepted, the policyholder will have to decide whether the payment offered is just or whether the insurance company is "low balling" and should be required to pay a higher benefit. Once the policyholder accepts the benefit offered by the company, he or she will have to sign a *release*. A signed release terminates all further claims or rights the policyholder may have against the insurance company. Or to put it another way, when a release is signed, the insurance company check is considered as payment in full.

Enforcing the Claim

If you are dissatisfied with the rejection of the claim or the benefits that the insurance company offers to pay, you will have to take action. There are many options, including:

Pursue Policies Remedies. The adjuster's decision is not necessarily the last word on the subject of the claim. Insurance companies always have an internal method of handling disputes with policyholders. For example, the matter may be handled informally by meeting with the adjuster's superiors and/or writing a letter of complaint. That may be sufficient to have the matter reviewed by the company, after which a better result may be obtained.

If that doesn't work, the policyholder should refer to the policy to see what remedies are found in the contract to settle disputes. Often, *arbitration* is the method provided for in the contract. An arbitration is similar to a trial except that it does not happen in court in front of a judge or jury but rather in an office of a private person known as an arbitrator. An arbitration hearing can settle the matter with little fuss or bother. However, some arbitration clauses are stacked in favor of the insurance company, which is not surprising since the company's lawyers wrote the terms of the policy.

File a Lawsuit. If the dispute with the company remains unsettled pursuant to policy remedies, a lawsuit may have to be brought. (Some policies may forbid lawsuits, making arbitration the sole remedy.) The lawsuit will usually charge the company with *breach of contract*; that is, the company will be charged with breaking its promises made in the insurance policy. The remedy for breach of contract is restricted to forcing the company to pay the money that is owed.

Sometimes insurance company conduct in denying valid claims is so outrageous that the policyholder may be able to sue the company for more than breach of contract. These suits are known as *bad faith cases.* If successful, bad faith cases permit the policyholder not only to be paid the amount of benefits owed, but to obtain compensation far beyond that available for breach of contract. Most notable among these remedies is the right to *punitive damages,* money awarded to punish the company for intentional and malicious wrong doing.

In real life, it is difficult to sue insurance companies. First, the policyholder may have to hire a lawyer, and pay court costs, which can be very expensive. Second, insurance companies are rich, powerful institutions. If one chooses to fight, the cost and time spent in the litigation may be prohibitive. Thus, many policyholders decide to settle for less than they believe they are entitled to. (If the claim is small, a policyholder might consider bringing an action against the company in small claims court, where a lawyer will not be needed and the matter can be brought quickly with little expense.)*

Report the Company. Insurance companies are regulated by each state. This regulatory scheme allows consumers another avenue of redress when their company doesn't pay benefits or cancels a policy without legal justification.

State insurance departments act as insurance cops on the beat and investigate many consumer complaints, including:

- Improper denial of claims
- Unreasonable delays in settling claims
- Illegal cancellation or termination of policies
- Misappropriation of funds paid in trust to an agent or broker
- Premium disputes, such as a raise without apparent cause

Policyholders with complaints should contact their insurance department and ask for complaint forms. (The phone number can be found in your phone book's blue pages in the state government section.) Once the complaint form is received, it should be carefully and fully filled out, with copies of all supporting documentation sent with the complaint to add to the complaint's credibility. (Remember, the state insurance department is a bureaucracy, and an improper or incomplete complaint may get lost in the shuffle or delayed if every "I" isn't

---

* For more information, see *Small Claims Court: Making Your Way Through the System,* by Theresa Meehan Rudy in Association with HALT, Random House, 1990. $8.95.

dotted or "T" crossed.) Also, be sure and send a copy of the complaint letter to the insurance company. In a few cases, complaining to the state may in and of itself be enough to break the impasse between company and policyholder.

Guarantee Funds. Unfortunately, from time to time insurance companies go out of business or become "insolvent." This can leave policyholders holding the bag for their own losses that would otherwise be covered by insurance.

Most states have guarantee funds to protect policyholders from losing money because a company has gone belly-up. Money in the funds comes from the insurance companies themselves. The funds will pay for most benefits that would otherwise be lost. Any questions about guarantee funds should be directed to the state insurance department.

THE INS AND OUTS OF SPECIFIC POLICIES

Each type of insurance policy has different contractual issues to be concerned with. Here is a summary:

Health Insurance

Health insurance may be the most important type of insurance for the protection of self and family. Unfortunately, health insurance may also be the most difficult to obtain. That is because health insurance companies "cherry pick;" that is, they seek to insure healthy and young people while denying insurance to older people or those with a history of health problems. This often means that people with chronic conditions, such as diabetes, or people who have survived life threatening diseases, such as cancer or heart attack, cannot obtain insurance unless they work for a large employer which has the clout to buy a group policy (one policy that covers many people) that provides benefits for all employees, come what may.

Purchasers of health insurance should be wary of the following policy exclusions and conditions:

Waiting periods. Often there are waiting periods before health insurance goes into effect. Any medical bills incurred during this period will not be covered.

Pre-existing Condition Exclusions. Many policies will exclude from coverage health problems that developed before the policy went into effect. Thus, a woman who has had surgery for ovarian cysts may find that her reproductive system is excluded from coverage in the policy for an extended period of time, or perhaps for the life of the policy.

Surgery and Hospitalization Preapproval Clauses. Many companies require policyholders to receive preapproval or obtain a second opinion before undergoing surgery or being hospitalized. Failure to comply with these clauses (except in a life-threatening emergency) could result in a substantial reduction of benefits.

There are two basic types of health insurance: traditional fee-for-service policies and health maintenance organizations (HMOs).

Fee-for-Service Policies. Most people are familiar with fee-for-service policies, such as Blue Cross. Fee-for-service policies are usually broken down into two sections: hospitalization and surgical/medical. The hospitalization portion of the policy pays for part or all of the costs of a hospital stay. (Watch out for waiting periods before coverage begins.) Major medical pays for doctors' treatment and surgery. There is usually a deductible in major medical policies (money the patient pays up-front before coverage kicks in) and a copayment (money the patient pays for medical care not paid by insurance). A typical policy has a $500 deductible with the patient paying 20% of covered costs after the deductible has been paid.

Fee-for-service health insurance has many consumer benefits, the primary one being that the patient has the right to choose his or her own doctors anywhere in the country. But these policies also have drawbacks, such as the cost, the fact that many policies exclude preventive care and prescription medication from coverage, and benefit caps that limit the lifetime liability of the insurance company to an amount specified in the policy. (Those with insurance with low maximum benefits may wish to purchase an additional major medical policy to protect against the very high costs of treating catastrophic injury and illness.)

HMOs. HMOs are a cost-cutting type of insurance, where the policyholder pays a premium and, in return, receives all necessary medical care from the HMO. This sounds great but there is a catch. The policyholder can only use HMO-approved doctors, clinics and hospitals. Failure to do so will relieve the HMO of paying any benefits, except in life-threatening emergencies. Also, the policyholder's primary care physician must approve referrals to a specialist, and then the specialist must be approved by the HMO. HMOs usually pay for preventive care and prescriptions.

Because health insurance is so expensive and because individuals may have a difficult time obtaining good coverage, most Americans obtain their health coverage under a group policy purchased by an employer or union. But what happens if the employee loses his or her job or there is a divorce or the employee dies? Is the employee and divorced or widowed spouse simply out of luck? Happily, the answer is no, thanks to an important law known as COBRA (for Congressional Omnibus Budget Reconciliation Act).

COBRA protects the health insurance coverage of laid-off workers, divorced and widowed spouses of covered workers, and others from losing their health insurance benefits. The law provides that laid-off workers may, at their own cost, convert the group coverage into their own name for a period of 18 months. Divorced and widowed spouses are protected for three years, as are children who have become adults and therefore have ceased to be protected by their parents' group policy.

The benefits of invoking COBRA are many:

- There are no pre-existing condition clauses or waiting periods, because the insurance never lapses.
- The premium will be lower, because it will be computed at the group rate rather than the more expensive individual rate.
- Treatment being received can continue without interruption.

Health insurance is virtually a necessity of life, yet 37 million Americans do not have health insurance. There is currently a move to institute some form of national health insurance policy that will provide coverage for everyone.

Auto Insurance

Everyone who owns a car is required by law in each state to have auto insurance or some other proof of financial responsibility, such as a bond. Law notwithstanding, and the potential costs of an accident being quite high, it is important for everyone who owns or leases a car to have their automobiles insured.

The typical automobile insurance policy consists of the following:

Liability Protection. This part of the policy protects the policyholder from liability for bodily injury that might be caused others due to negligent driving. The policy will usually have a split-limit amount, such as $50,000/$100,000. The first figure represents the maximum each injured person is entitled to receive and the later figure the maximum amount the company will pay per accident, no matter how many people are injured. Most states set the minimum amount of liability insurance at $15,000/$30,000, although some states require higher coverage and some lower. (Ask your insurance agent for the minimum requirements in your state.)

Property Damage. This portion of the policy compels the insurance company to pay for property damaged by the policyholder, such as another car or a fence. Like coverage for personal injury, the policy will provide maximum benefits that the insurance has to pay. Many states require minimum coverage of $10,000 or so, but in this age where even the least expensive cars can cost $10,000, that may not be enough to fully protect the policyholder's assets.

Cost of Defense. The liability portion of the policy also requires the company to pay for the cost of lawyers and court costs in the event that the insured is sued for damages.

Medical Pay. This optional coverage pays for the medical bills (and funeral expenses) of the insured, his or her family, or a passenger in the insured car that is injured or killed in an accident. The Medical Pay portion of the policy pays benefits regardless of which driver is at fault.

Uninsured Motorist. This optional coverage protects the insured for personal injury damages caused by an uninsured (or in some cases, underinsured) driver. This protection is based on fault. If the insured driver caused the accident with the uninsured driver, the company will deny the claim. (This is important protection. Fully ⅓ of all drivers in some areas of the country are uninsured.)

Uninsured motorist protection is a split-limit scheme, similar to liability protection. To collect benefits for injuries caused by an uninsured driver, the policyholder must make a claim against his or her own insurance company. Thereafter, if there is a dispute, there will be an arbitration to determine what, if any benefits are owed.

Collision and Comprehensive Coverage. Collision protection protects the insured's vehicle and compels the company to pay for repairs or the fair market value of the vehicle, when it is involved in an accident. This coverage is not based on fault. (Collision coverage is optional. Many people with older cars do not take out collision coverage because the benefits would be too low to make premium payments worthwhile.)

Comprehensive coverage is similar to collision coverage except that it protects against losses from theft, damage from falling objects, and other such occurrences. It too is optional coverage not based on fault.

Both collision and comprehensive coverages require a deductible from the insured.

A word about no-fault insurance: Fourteen states have some version of "no-fault" insurance. No-fault is designed to reduce court congestion and the price of auto insurance by eliminating smaller cases from the tort system. The idea is for anyone who has been injured to receive benefits from his or her own insurance company for lost wages and medical bills, even if he or she caused the accident. In return, the injured person gives up the right to sue in small cases and the right to receive dollar payment for the pain that has or will be suffered. However, many states have limits on the amount of wage losses that can be collected. (New York's is 80% of the lost wage with a cap of $2,000 per month. Minnesota's is lower, only being $250 per week.)

Auto insurance policies in fault and no-fault states are similar, although no-fault insurance will have a personal injury policy section (PIP) that defines the company's obligation in the event a no-fault claim is made. People still need liability coverage because larger accidents do not come under the no-fault provisions of the law.

Homeowner's Insurance

Homeowner's insurance is designed to protect homeowners from damage to property and personal liability for negligence.

Five basic areas are protected in the property section of a homeowner's policy:

- The dwelling
- Other structures on the property
- Personal property
- Loss of use
- Miscellaneous coverages

Homeowner's policies protect against damages caused by fire, lightning, windstorm, theft, riot, vandalism and damage cause by vehicles. The basic policy may or may not cover losses due to the weight of snow, falling objects, defects, and damage caused by electrical malfunctions, depending on the type of policy that is purchased.

It is important to know what is and is not covered by the policy. For example, the following are common exclusions from coverage:

- Loss cause by collapse of the structure due to faulty construction or geological shifts or earthquake. (Earthquake coverage can be purchased at an extra price.)
- Freezing, when the dwelling is vacant.
- Vandalism if the dwelling has been vacant for 30 days.
- Constant or repeated water seepage.

- Water damage, including flood, tidal wave or backed-up sewers. (Flood insurance can be purchased in some areas.)
- Power failure.
- Negligence or intentional damage caused by the insured.
- War.

The personal property protection will also be limited unless extra coverage is purchased. For example, a basic policy only covers the loss of up to $200 in money and $1,000 for losses due to theft of jewelry, watches, furs, or precious stones. (Again, extra protection can be purchased at an additional price.)

The liability section of the policy protects the insured against the costs of damages caused by his or her own negligence, whether the injury was caused on the property or off. This portion of the policy, like an auto insurance policy, also covers the cost of attorneys and court costs in the event the insured is sued.

The liability section also has exclusions, including:

- Intentional acts of the insured.
- Bodily injury to the insured.
- Damage arising out of business activities or the providing of professional services.
- Damages caused by the operation of a vehicle, a watercraft or an aircraft.
- The passing of communicable diseases.
- Injuries covered by workers' compensation.

Renter's insurance is similar to homeowner's insurance, with the exception that it will not protect against destruction of the premises, which is, of course, the responsibility of the property owner.

Life Insurance

The life insurance contract, in its essence, is very simple. A person's life is insured. If that person dies, those named in the policy as beneficiaries receive an amount of money specified in the insurance contract. The person who takes out the policy, usually but not necessarily the insured, is the owner of the policy who has the right to name beneficiaries, cancel the policy, and otherwise control its management.

The above description applies to term life insurance policies. Term policies are those taken out for a specific term. If the insured dies while the policy is in effect, the policy must pay benefits. If the contract lapses, the business relationship between owner, beneficiaries, insured and the insurance company terminates.

Things get a little complicated when life insurance is also used as an investment vehicle. These policies are known generically as cash value life insurance. The life insurance company charges a higher premium than it does for term life policies. The excess money, minus costs and commissions, is then invested by the life insurance company and the return accrues cash value. This cash value can be borrowed against and must be returned to the owner of the policy if the insurance is cancelled.

Cash value life insurance has certain unique tax benefits:

The Value That Accrues Is Tax Deferred. If someone opens a bank savings account, the income that accrues is subject to income tax. This is also true of the increased value in cash value policies. However, the tax is deferred until the policy is cashed by the owner of the policy. Moreover, if a tax is due, the policyholder can deduct the price of premiums from the cash value received, thereby reducing or eliminating the tax. Also, if policy benefits are paid due to the death of the insured, the cash value merges with the benefit and no taxes are owed.

Money Borrowed Against the Cash Value Is Not Taxed. This gives the owner of a cash value policy access to cash with no tax consequences. However, borrowing against the cash value may affect the benefit, and if the money is not repaid, the policy may lapse.

Both term life insurance and cash value life insurance proceeds paid to beneficiaries are not subject to income taxes. They are also usually not subject to inheritance taxes unless the beneficiary is the dead person's estate.

That closes our discussion of the legalities surrounding personal insurance. There is much more to learn about the ins and outs of individual policies than can be presented here. To learn more, contact your insurance agent or company representative, and read one of the many books on insurance, some which are listed in the bibliography.

14

MANAGING YOUR MONEY & ESTATE

In these days of high taxes and a faltering economy, it is more important than ever for families to take special care in managing their money and estate. Two main areas to be concerned about are: dealing with money issues during life and planning what will happen after death. This chapter will cover both areas, including a description of the laws of credit, banking, and pensions, and some estate planning techniques, such as the use of wills and trusts.

MANAGING YOUR BUSINESS AFFAIRS

First, let's discuss the important issues surrounding a family's personal business affairs. Primarily, this discussion will address the laws of credit, pension plans and banking. We start with that all-American institution: the credit card.

The Law of Credit

There are two basic types of credit: open-ended lines of credit and closed-ended lines of credit.

Open-ended Credit. Credit cards are an open-ended type line of credit, meaning a specific amount is not being borrowed but a line of credit is extended by the lender which the cardholder is able to use up to a predefined limit.

Closed-ended Credit. A typical example of a closed-ended type of credit is an auto loan, where a specific amount is borrowed and repaid over a defined period of time.

The terms of every credit agreement are defined in the credit agreement. For example, a credit card agreement will establish, among other terms, the credit limit, the amount of interest that will be charged, the manner in which the minimum monthly payment is determined, the right of the credit card company to withdraw the card, and penalties for late payment or default. You will also receive with your credit card cardholder agreement information about special cardholder privileges, such as discounts on car rentals or buyer protection plans.

The Fair Credit Reporting Act (FCRA). Credit card companies and other lending institutions report on your payment record, credit limit and current balance to businesses known as credit reporting bureaus. Other lenders and credit card companies, in turn, rely on the information stored in a computer data base by the credit bureau to help them determined your credit worthiness. Creditors do not need your permission to access your credit history from the credit bureau, nor do they need to notify you that they have taken such action.

Under the *Fair Credit Reporting Act,* anyone who is turned down for credit, based on information in their credit report has to be told where the credit report was obtained. You have the right to request a free copy of your credit report, if the request is made within 30 days of being turned down. (Credit reports can be purchased at any time. Also, TRW, one of the nation's largest credit bureaus, offers free credit reports once per year.) This right can be exercised by writing to the credit reporting bureau that the credit company relied upon when deciding whether to turn down your credit application. The name and address of the credit reporting company must be supplied to you by the credit card company or lender in the rejection notice. Under the *Equal Credit Opportunity Act (ECOA),* you have the right to know why your credit was denied. The creditor has to list, in writing, the specific reasons you were denied credit or it must give you a telephone number to call from which to get that information.

You also have the right to dispute information in your credit report that you believe is inaccurate or incomplete. This is typically done by writing a letter to the credit reporting company identifying the mistakes and asking the company to correct its records. When a letter is written, the credit reporting company is legally required to verify the information with the lender that reported it. If it cannot verify the information, it is legally required to remove it from the report. You have the legal right to have corrected credit reports sent to all credit companies and lenders which have requested a credit report on you during the previous six months. Some credit bureaus will allow you to add a statement to your files explaining why you believe information is inaccurate.

Here is a sample letter:

Acme Credit Reporting Bureau
50 Blewit Square
Mistake, Oklahoma 11111

RE: Credit Report Dated October 12, 1993

To Whom It May Concern:

On October 13, 1993, your company issued a credit report on me to Ajax MasterCard. I have enclosed a copy of this report.

This report contains erroneous information. Specifically, the following mistakes occurred:

1) I have never borrowed money from Usury Credit Corporation as the report states. Therefore, I can never have been late in making payments to that company.

2) I was late in paying my account to Just Debt Finance in April and May, 1992. The reason I was late with the payments is that my home was destroyed in a fire and there was a period of time when my personal financial affairs were in a state of confusion. I did make up all late payments and, in fact, have paid that debt in full. Would you please reflect the cause for the late payments in the future.

Once you have investigated and verified the above, please notify all parties who have requested my credit report from you in the last six months and send me written proof that you have done so.

Very truly yours,

Mary Informed

Your good credit record is one of the most important personal "assets" you own. That being so, it is up to you to use the laws available to protect it.

Women and Credit

Under the Equal Credit Opportunity Act (ECOA), women have the right to apply for credit without fear of discrimination on the basis of gender, marital status, age or national origin. This means that the only basis for denying credit must be an objective finding of credit unworthiness based on credit history, income and other such considerations. Among the legal benefits of the ECOA are the following:

- It gives married women a credit history. Under the ECOA, credit grantors must report credit history of joint accounts in both spouse's names.
- If marital status changes, that fact alone cannot be the basis for revoking credit privileges. However, the creditor can compel the applicant to fill out a new application if credit has been based on the former spouse's income.
- The statistical likelihood of having children cannot be used to deny credit.
- The husband need not sign the credit card application. Nor can a husband's co-signing (agreeing to be responsible for the debt in the event of default) be required as a condition of extending credit.

Correcting Billing Errors

Many people mistakenly believe that credit companies never make mistakes in their billing. This can be an expensive belief. Computers notwithstanding, mistakes happen and you are the only one who will be there to catch them.

The Fair Credit Billing Act has given consumers the right to correct mistakes on their credit card bills and has established the manner in which such mistakes are to be handled. That procedure is as follows:

- If you believe a mistake has been made, you must notify your creditor. That notification must be *in writing* within 60 days of the date the statement on which the charge appeared was sent to you. Telephone calls do not protect your rights.
- The credit card or loan company then must acknowledge the letter of complaint within 30 days.
- While waiting for a reply from the credit card company, you do not have to pay the amount in dispute. However, amounts not in dispute must be paid according to the terms of the credit agreement.
- The creditor has two billing periods, or 90 days, whichever comes sooner, to resolve the matter. If the company does not follow the law in resolving the complaint, it may be required to forfeit the first $50 of the charge, even if the original bill was not in error.
- Once the credit card company says you're wrong and you haven't paid promptly, it can report delinquent payments to credit bureaus.

Rebecca applied for credit with MasterCard. She was rejected based on a credit bureau's report that she had gone bankrupt. This was false. Rebecca's former husband had gone bankrupt.

Rebecca wrote the credit bureau and obtained a copy of her credit report. The bureau report showed a bankruptcy, but it also showed that she was current on all her bills. Rebecca wrote the reporting company and demanded that the false report be corrected. The reporting company investigated and found that an error had indeed been made. The company then sent a letter to the credit card company correcting its mistake. Rebecca contacted MasterCard and asked it to reconsider its rejection. The credit bureau report now corrected, Rebecca received her credit card.

Rebecca used the credit card. However, a $100 charge was charged as $1000. Rebecca was aghast at the mistake and wrote the company demanding they correct the error. She included a photocopy of her receipt for the charge, proving the original charge was $100. MasterCard corrected the mistake.

Withholding Payment to Retailers

If there's a problem with merchandise paid for by credit card, you may be able to withhold payment until the matter is resolved, thanks to the *Truth-in-Lending Act.* This law gives consumers important leverage. If a consumer receives defective merchandise purchased by credit card, *payment may be withheld to the credit card company* for the merchandise—if the consumer makes a good faith effort to resolve the matter directly with the merchant.

In order for the right to apply, the goods purchased must exceed $50 in value and the sale must have taken place within 100 miles of your current address.

There are many other issues involving credit card usage that are consumer-oriented rather than legal. How do you get lower interest rates? What is the best way to manage credit? Are there any cards that do not have annual fees? These questions and more can be addressed by the nonprofit organization Bankcard Holders of America, an activist and educational association for credit card consumers. For more information contact them by writing: Bankcard Holders of America, 560 Herndon Parkway, Ste. 120, Herndon, VA 22070, or by calling (703) 481-1110.

If you get into credit card trouble, you can contact the Consumer Credit Counseling Service, a nonprofit organization. CCCS will put you on a budget and attempt to arrange for your creditors to work with you should you get in over your head. There are local CCCS branches in most major cities. Its telephone number can be found in the white pages of your telephone book. Or, you can contact: The National Foundation for Consumer Credit, 8611 Second Ave., Ste. 100, Silver Spring, MD 20910. The organization can also be reached at (301) 589-5600 or call (800) 388-CCCS for a national referral.

PENSION PLANS

This section addresses what you need to know about pensions and individual retirement accounts (IRAs).

You don't need to read this book to know that pensions are important. Receiving a pension can make the difference between an enjoyable and comfortable retirement and living on the edge of financial instability.

Pensions generally fall into two types: *defined benefit* and *defined contribution* plans.

Defined Benefit Plans

The defined benefit plan is probably the most common pension system and the easiest to understand. In a defined benefit plan, the worker is guaranteed a specific amount per month for each year of service, or, perhaps, the pension benefit is based on a defined percentage of the worker's average salary over the years. Whichever it is, the amount of the pension is based on an established formula, hence the term, defined benefit.

Defined Contribution Plans

In a defined contribution pension, unlike the defined benefit plan, the amount of money that the worker will receive upon retirement is not guaranteed. Rather, the employer promises to contribute a specified amount into the pension plan itself. That is the extent of the employer's responsibility. The money is then invested by the administrators of the pension fund. When the worker retires, the benefit will be based on the amount the employer has contributed to the plan and the amount of money the plan has earned over the years investing that money. Upon retirement, the worker can elect to receive his or her pension in monthly payments or a lump sum. Pending retirement, the employee can request an individual benefit statement to find out what the accrued benefit is to date.

Vesting

In order to collect pension dollars, you must be *vested* in the program. This means that you must meet the plan's established requirements that give rise to your legal right to receive pension benefits. Vesting rules will be summarized in a booklet you will receive from your pension system describing your pension and your rights in the program.

Vesting can be total, meaning you are entitled to receive 100% of the pension benefits. Partial vesting means that you are entitled to a percentage of total benefits. If you leave the job before vesting, you will receive no pension and any money contributed on your behalf into the system will remain with the pension plan. Thus, it is important that you understand the vesting rules of your plan before you decide to leave your job.

Integrated Plans

Integrated pension plans offer less than they seem to promise on the surface. Integrated pension plans boast that they will guarantee you a certain percentage of your working monthly income when you retire. The level promised is called the "goal." Here's the catch. Your pension will be integrated with your Social Security to achieve the goal. That often means the more you earn in Social Security, the less you will be paid in pension benefits. As a result, workers with integrated plans usually receive lower pension benefits than they would have received if their plan did not have an integration clause, since the plan's payments are lowered every time your Social Security goes up.

Federal Law and Your Pension

Private pension plans are governed by the federal law called the Employee Retirement Income Security Act (ERISA), which, along with other federal statutes, protects your pension rights. Here are some of the important protections afforded by the law:

Your Right to Receive Information About the Plan Is Guaranteed. ERISA establishes your right to ask for and receive a "Summary Plan Description," which will describe:

- How your plan works.
- Your options for collecting benefits.
- The rules of participation.
- How your benefits accrue.
- How your rights vest.
- Your choice for other benefits, such as early retirement or payments to your spouse if you die.
- Your right to request an individual benefit's statement— contact your plan administrator for further details.

Annual Reports Must Be Made to the Government. ERISA requires each plan governed by the law to make a yearly report to the government detailing the financial investments made by the plan. You have a right to receive a copy of this report. The report is referred to as the I.R.S. Form 5500.

The Law Protects Your Accrued Pension Credits. At one time, an extensive illness or work lay-off could have led to the loss of your accrued pension benefits, interfering with your rights to vest. Federal law now protects accrued benefits. Called the *break-in-service rules*, under the law you cannot lose your accrued pension credits unless you are off of work for five or more years.

> Liam worked for a major corporation. He worked for two years, accruing pension rights under the corporation's pension plan. The recession hit and Liam was laid off. He was not called back to work for one year. When Liam returned to work, his boss told him that he had lost all pension credits and would have to begin again to accrue pension credits toward vesting. But Liam knew that under the law, he could not have his accrued pension credits taken from him unless he had been out of work for five or more years. He pointed out the law to his employer and soon had all of his pension credits restored.

Your Vesting Rights Cannot Be Changed. Once you have your rights vested under an existing plan, they cannot be withdrawn or reduced by a change in the vesting rules of your plan.

Pension plans are generally well-managed and financially healthy. However, some pension funds have gone broke. If yours goes broke, what happens? You may have rights to at least partial payment with the Pension Benefit Guaranty Corporation. If your plan has gone belly-up, the Guaranty Corporation can be reached at 2020 K St., N.W., Washington D.C. 20006, or by calling (202) 788-8800 to find out whether you qualify for benefits.

Individual Retirement Accounts

IRAs are middle-class tax shelters that permit people to save for retirement and save money on income taxes. If you open an

IRA account, you can deposit $2,000, or 100 percent of your earned income—whichever is less—per year into an account and you may be able to deduct the amount invested, depending on your individual circumstances.

The deductibility of the investment may be affected by your participation in another pension plan. In 1993, if you participated in another retirement plan and earned less than $25,000, your contribution was fully deductible. If you earned between $25,000–$30,000, a partial deduction is allowed, and over $30,000, no deductible is allowed.

Your marital status can also affect the deductibility of your contribution. If you're married and your spouse participates in another retirement plan, the government considers both of you as covered by that plan. Your deduction could be reduced or eliminated, depending on your adjusted gross income.

Interest earned on IRAs is tax-deferred. That means you will not have to pay a tax on the interest as it accrues. When you withdraw money from your IRA, you will pay tax on the proceeds you withdraw.

The rules of IRAs are continually changing. So before you take any major step regarding your IRA, be sure to consult the IRS, your tax advisor or an official of a bank or other financial institution who is knowledgeable about IRA matters.

BANKING

Banking for the average consumer has become complicated. And, as the recent savings and loan debacle has shown, banking may be more risky. That being so, keep the following in mind when conducting your banking business.

Make Sure Your Institution Is Safe

The law helps you make sure your money is safe when you bank. Of primary importance is the *Federal Deposit Insurance Corporation* (FDIC). A bank that is insured by the FDIC protects your deposits to a maximum of $100,000 per account. If you bank at an insured bank that fails, eventually you will receive your funds up to the maximum amount. On the other hand, if you bank at a thrift institution that is not insured (they often offer higher interest rates), you are probably out of luck. (That is one reason why the S & L crisis will be so expensive. Depositors at failed institutions were covered by insurance.)

Rules Concerning Deposits

The kind of account you select will dictate your rights under the account agreement with your bank. For example, interest will usually be paid on savings accounts and certificates of deposits (CDs). (A savings account, also known as a passbook account, allows you unlimited access to your money. A CD will tie up your money for the length of time the CD remains in effect. The interest rate of a CD will be higher but early withdrawal will cost you an interest penalty.)

When comparing deposits, note the differences in the way interest is computed. Look at the *annual percentage yield* (APY) of the account, as opposed to the more familiar *annual percentage rate* (APR). The APY applied to your deposit balance gives you the amount of money in interest you would earn over one year if you held your deposit balance constant. Many banks advertise based on APR, which is merely the interest rate at a point in time, and does not take into account the manner in which interest is compounded (earns interest on interest). (For example, some accounts compound interest daily, which earns more money than accounts that compound monthly.) By comparing the APYs of various accounts, you will get a better idea about which account will actually earn you more money.

Compare Fees

All banks charge fees for the services they provide. For example, if you bounce a check, you will have to pay the bank a fee. Many banks also charge fees for administering checking accounts, balance inquiries, and the cost of check printing. (The fees will be set forth in your banking agreement.) Be sure you understand a bank's fee structure before you agree to use the bank's services.

Credit Unions

Credit unions are nonprofit, cooperatively-owned organizations created to promote thrift among the union's members and to provide low-cost loans. Credit unions are often organized to serve a specific group of people. For example, many government employees have a credit union. So do many labor unions or large, privately-owned companies. Presently, about 50 million people belong to credit unions.

Credit unions are regulated and insured like banks. They are also subject to failure if not managed carefully. Thus, even though you are likely to earn a higher annual yield and be able to obtain lower levels of interest on loans, be as careful when looking for a credit union as you are when choosing a bank.

PLANNING FOR YOUR DEMISE

An important part of maintaining your estate is taking the steps necessary to keep it intact after you die. This is accomplished in a legal process known as *estate planning*. The primary tools available in estate planning are wills and trusts. Wills also allow parents to designate who they wish to be the guardians of their minor children should they die.

Formal Wills

Everyone needs a will. If you die without one, you lose control over who gets your property. You will be unable to give specific items to specific people, since your entire estate will be distributed to your *heirs* (those who are legally allowed to inherit from you) as provided by law.

As stated above, a will also allows you to name whom you want to take care of your minor children. You also name the person you want to distribute your property and pay your bills should you die (the *executor*). It even allows you to "disinherit" anyone you do not want to receive property.

Each state has its own laws regarding the validity of wills and how they are to be probated (the legal process of concluding a deceased person's affairs). Wills can be simple or complex, even handwritten, in some cases. You can write your own will or have an attorney do it on your behalf. However, the rules of wills are arcane and precise. Thus, it is a good idea to read a detailed summary of the law before attempting to write your own.*

Trusts

A trust is a legal entity created by law that can own, hold and pay out assets (money and property) that are given to it. You establish a trust by signing a document that creates the trust entity and then by transferring title of the property you are placing in trust into the trust itself. At that point, you no longer own the property—the trust does.

Different trusts accomplish different goals. Trusts can be set up to provide for a child's education, to take care of a dependent spouse, to restrict the amount of money a spendthrift relative receives, to hold and distribute insurance proceeds, to avoid probate and even to avoid paying taxes. Trusts can be created during life (known as an *inter vivos* or *living trust*) or after death (a *testamentary trust*).

The most popular trust, the revocable living trust, avoids probate and can be prepared without a lawyer if you take the time and care to do it right. Other trusts are more complex, such as the charitable or irrevocable trust, and probably require a lawyer's assistance to establish.

---

* For more details on the law of wills and how to write your own, see HALT's book *Wills: A Do-It-Yourself Guide.*

15

TAKING CARE
OF OLDER PARENTS

Nearly 20 percent of all seniors—5.7 million people—are living below or near the poverty line. Surprisingly, 1.9 million of these seniors do not receive any federal assistance. Many of these seniors need help providing for their own care. So do seniors who have health problems or who have been sufficiently afflicted by "old age" that they can no longer adequately provide for all of their own needs.

As a result, an increasing number of adult children are having to step in and provide care for their own parents. These caregivers, often called the "sandwich generation" because they are responsible for both older parents and minor children, have a lot on their plate. There is much to know about. What are the options for senior housing? What help is available? Is there a way to obtain legal control of the assets of parents who can no longer care for their own affairs?

This chapter will answer these questions and discuss the most pressing issues facing families with seniors who need help with their own care. For additional information on issues involving seniors, such as Social Security, Medicare and the like, see Appendix 4, the bibliography.

THE LEGAL OBLIGATION TO CARE FOR PARENTS

Many states require the adult children of indigent parents to help pay for their support, based on the idea of reciprocity—that is, the parent was obliged to support the child and it is only fair that the reverse be true in times of special need. However, with Social Security, Supplemental Security Income and other general welfare programs available to assist indigent seniors, the issue of a child's obligation to support his or her parents is rarely before the courts. In one such case, the California Supreme Court, in 1973, upheld a court order requiring adult children to pay parent support to help reimburse the state for state aid given the parents. (*Swoap v. Superior Court of Sacramento County.*)

Nevertheless, many adult children want to care for their parents. The rest of this chapter deals with the options that families have when a senior is in need of assistance.

HOUSING OPTIONS OTHER THAN NURSING HOMES

One myth that worries older people and their families is the false belief that the only option for seniors who can no longer live independently is the nursing home. Thankfully, that is not true. There are many other options available, especially if the senior does not need the kind of intense assistance that is provided by nursing homes.

Living at Home

Many seniors who are finding it difficult to live independently could continue to live in their own home if they received some assistance. What many families don't realize is that such help can be available at low or no cost.

If it is medical assistance that is required, home health care benefits from Medicare may pay for it. Thanks to Medicare cost-cutting resulting in seniors being discharged from hospitals earlier than was once the case, home health care has become a growth industry. Many medical conditions once treated in the hospital, such as recuperation from surgery, are now often handled at home for a lower price tag, while providing a better healing environment for the patient.

Medicare offers unlimited home health benefits under the following specified conditions:

- The care must include periodically provided skilled nursing care (such as changing surgical dressings, giving injections, physical therapy or speech therapy).
- The senior must be home-bound.
- The senior must be under the care of a physician who prescribes home health care.
- The doctor must establish the home health care plan.
- The home health care agency must participate in Medicare.

Home health care does not cover assistance known as custodial care, e.g., housekeeping, cooking or other matters of personal living. In fact, Medicare will *not* pay for such services, nor will Medicaid when the custodial care is provided in-home. Thus, providing such care will usually be the financial responsibility of the family or the senior requiring care.

There is some good news, however. Volunteers may be available in the community to assist seniors in their own homes. For example, the federally financed *Senior Companion Program* may be able to help. Senior Companion volunteers are senior citizens who literally become companions to other seniors who need their services. The volunteers perform all kinds of services, including letter writing, running errands, light housekeeping and most important, companionship. There is no charge for the service. (The program volunteers are low-income seniors who receive a small stipend for the work they perform.) Sometimes the extra attention provided by such volunteers, when combined with custodial care, and when necessary, home health care, is enough to permit a senior to remain in their own home. For more information on the Senior Companion Program, contact your local area agency on aging. (The United Way, the American Association of Retired Persons [AARP] and local churches may also have volunteer programs that could make the difference for a senior who wants to continue to live at home. For example, many local groups offer a "meals on wheels" type program that will deliver nutritious, low cost food to seniors on a daily basis.)

Sometimes the problem that threatens to force a senior out

of his or her own home is financial. It is not unusual for seniors to be "property rich" but "cash poor." For example, a senior who owns a home free-and-clear, may find it difficult to pay for in-home services or other expenses of life. Many in this circumstance believe their only option is to sell the property and move to a retirement home. But there may be another way: the *reverse mortgage* (also known as a "home equity conversion").

A reverse mortgage is a home loan but a loan with a big difference—a difference that can allow seniors to continue to live comfortably in their own homes. Here's how the reverse mortgage works:

- A loan is granted with length and amount of money based on the equity in the senior's home. (The equity is the difference between the fair market value of the home and any mortgage on the property.)
- Instead of receiving a lump sum of money, the senior receives monthly payments from the mortgage lender.
- Depending on the terms, the payments will be paid for the senior's life or until the equity has been eaten up by payments.
- The senior does not make house payments.
- The loan must be paid upon the death of the senior or when the senior permanently leaves the home. Usually, this means the property is sold.

The beauty of a reverse mortgage is that it allows a substantial income to seniors, while permitting them to remain home without being encumbered by house payments. For many seniors, this added income can be "just what the doctor ordered," allowing them to pay for custodial care and other services permitting them to remain at home.

Reverse mortgages are a relatively new lending plan and may not be available in all locales. For more information, contact the AARP, which can send you a free copy of a reverse mortgage information pamphlet called "Home-made Money." It also has a list of reverse mortgage lenders available at no cost for single copies. This information can be obtained by contacting: AARP Home Equity Information Center, 601 E St., NW, Washington D.C. 20049; telephone (202) 434-3525.

Living With an Adult Child

Adult children of seniors may want to have a parent live with them but may wonder how that will be accomplished if the parent needs care. Here are some options:

ECHO Housing. Sometimes adult children want to have an aging parent live with them but simply don't have the room. ECHO housing may be the answer.

The anagram "ECHO" stands for Elder Cottage Housing Opportunity. ECHO cottages are small temporary living quarters that are installed on the property of a single family residence. The cottages can be removed when no longer needed.

ECHO housing may not be for everybody. For one thing, they are expensive—costing between $17,000 and $33,000. For another, many yards will be too small to accommodate the cottages, which range in size between 300 and 720 square feet. Moreover, issues such as sewer connection and local zoning restrictions may have to be addressed. However, an ECHO cottage has a significant advantage in that it allows both generations to live together while maintaining the privacy of each.

For more information on ECHO housing, contact: Coastal Colonial Corporation, 2935 Meadow View Rd., Manheim, PA 17545; telephone (717) 665-6761.

Community Care Programs. Most communities have many senior care programs that can assist families that care for partially dependent parents at home. They include:

Adult Day Care Centers. Adult day care centers help dependent adults so that their families can work and conduct personal business without worrying about their parent being left home alone.

Multi-Purpose Senior Centers. Senior centers provide companionship, recreation, informational lectures, and low-cost meals for seniors.

Transportation Programs. Many communities have transportation programs that can help relatively able seniors get around town without having to disrupt family work schedules or daily routine.

Respite Care. Occasionally, family caregivers need a short break from the sometimes arduous task of caring for a loved one. Many communities have respite care services that will care for the needy senior for a short time, allowing the rest of the family to take a vacation or get some rest.

For more information on these and other senior programs that may be available in your community, contact your the National Association of Area Agencies on Aging (NAAAA) at (800) 677-1116.

Hospice Care

If a family is caring for a parent who is suffering from a terminal illness, hospice care paid by Medicare can provide significant, compassionate assistance for both the senior and the family.

Hospice care is designed to treat the terminally ill, not to prolong life or bring about a cure, but to maintain the quality of life through pain control, symptom management and support services. Hospice care is usually but not always provided in the home.

Three conditions must be met for Medicare to pay for hospice treatment:

- The senior citizen's doctor must certify that the patient is terminally ill.
- The hospice care will be provided instead of standard Medicare benefits. (If the senior requires treatment for a malady not related to the terminal condition, Medicare will provide benefits for that other illness.)
- The hospice care provider must be a Medicare participating service provider.

Hospice care can provide very helpful services for a low cost if paid by Medicare. For more information on hospice treatment, contact your local Social Security office and ask for information on Medicare and hospice care.

Other Housing Options

There are a myriad of other housing options available for seniors. For example, retirement hotels allow seniors who are able to partially care for themselves to live in relative independence while having maid service, meals and other forms of assistance provided by the facility. Many communities permit group homes to provide care for seniors. A group home is a private residence where several seniors live, take meals, and receive assistance, partially cared for by the owner of the property who charges a fee for the service. Such homes must be licensed by the state.

With so many services available, it can be difficult to know which service providers are good and which bad. That being so, many families turn to experts who, for a fee, can refer their clients to the best care providers in a community, be it a nursing home, a board and care home, a geriatric specialist physician or a psychiatrist who specializes in treating the mental problems of seniors. These professionals are known as *private geriatric care managers.* The National Association of Professional Geriatric Care Managers (NAPGCM) can refer you to a care manager in your community. The association can be reached at NAPGCM, 655 N. Alvernon Way, Suite 108, Tuscon, AZ 85711; telephone (602) 881-8008.

NURSING HOMES

The biggest fear of many is that their parents will have to be admitted into a nursing home. In reality, most seniors never end up in nursing homes, and if they do, it is usually at an advanced age. For example, according to recent statistics, only one percent of senior citizens between the ages of 65–74 live in nursing homes. The percentage goes up for seniors between age 74 and 85—but only to 6 percent. Only when seniors live past 85 do 22% have to be placed into nursing homes. In fact, fully 42 percent of all nursing home beds are taken by people over the age of 85. Still, such statistics provide cold comfort when it is your parent who is the one who must be admitted into a nursing home.

The decision to place a parent into a nursing home is never an easy one. Nursing homes have the sometimes deserved reputations as warehouses for the old. In reality, most are very professionally administered by people who really care about the people they serve. Still, the horror stories of patients being abused or neglected and facilities that smell like a toilet are not all fiction. Sometimes poor care is provided, but less so for residents who have families who visit and who interact with the staff, who pay attention to the quality of care that is delivered and who know their rights. Thus, it behooves families with loved ones who must be admitted into a nursing home to understand the legal rights of residents and the nature of nursing home care.

What You Are Paying For

Nursing homes are not hospitals, nor are they skilled nursing centers, although skilled nursing may be provided. Rather, nursing homes are *custodial care* facilities that provide four basic services:

- Minor medical care, usually provided by the patient's own doctor. Thus, chronic conditions such as diabetes will be managed, minor treatments will be provided and the like.
- Nursing care, such as administering injections, performing catheterizations, etc., as ordered by a doctor.
- Personal care, such as assistance with walking, bathing, eating, and preparation of special diets.
- Residential services, including room, board, and a program of social activities.

The Rights of Nursing Home Patients

Many states have laws which guarantee the rights of nursing home patients. These rights generally include the following:

- The right to safe, considerate care.
- An environment which is clean, sanitary and in good repair.
- A diet consisting of a variety of good, quality foods.
- The existence of organized recreational activities.

- The right to privacy when visited by a spouse and the right to share a room if both spouses are residents of the facility.
- Liberal visiting hours.
- An environment where grievances may be presented without fear of reprisal.
- An environment which allows for freedom of religious expression and worship.
- An opportunity for the patient to purchase drugs and medical supplies from a pharmacy or other source of their choice.

These and other rights that may exist should be posted in the nursing home in a public place. If you don't see it, be sure to ask.

The Nursing Home Ombudsman

Nursing home patients have the right to complain and have their concerns taken seriously. Yet, many feel intimidated, being dependent for their care on the very people about whom they may have a complaint. For that reason, each state has created the office of state ombudsman.

The job of the ombudsman is to mediate problems that may arise between nursing homes and patients and/or patients' families. The men and women who perform this service are specially trained for the job and can usually pour oil on troubled waters. Contact your nursing home administration for the address and phone number of the ombudsman, or contact your local agency on aging.

Paying For Nursing Home Care

Medicare, the national insurance program for senior citizens, does not pay for most nursing home care. That means that nursing home patients and/or their families are responsible for the cost of care. That is an expensive proposition. Nursing homes cost about $2,500 per month.

With costs being as high as they are, many nursing home patients eventually run out of money. At that point, they must rely on Medicaid to pay for their care. Medicaid is a federally-assisted, state-administered health care program which aids the poor, including senior citizens. Every state except Arizona participates in the plan, although Arizona has a similar plan of its own.

To be eligible for Medicaid, a senior citizen must be in significant financial need—which usually means having very low income and little or no property. For older people who are in nursing homes, this often means using a lifetime of savings to pay for care—money the senior had hoped to leave to their loved ones.

To avoid losing all of their money to nursing home and other medical bills, many seniors plan ahead for Medicaid by placing their money into assets that are exempt from being counted when determining Medicaid eligibility. For example, the home of the Medicaid patient may be exempt, as may a car. Because Medicaid is an expensive government program, the law is continually changing as the government and lawyers who specialize in planning for Medicaid play leap-frog with each other over loopholes in the law.

Nursing homes who accept Medicaid (not all do) are not allowed to discriminate against Medicaid residents. However, in the real world, it isn't that simple. Private-paid patients pay the nursing homes more money than Medicaid residents for the same level of care. Thus, nursing homes want as many private-pay residents as they can get. For this reason, legal or not, Medicaid patients may find the better nursing homes have a waiting list and thus may end up in a lower-quality facility.

One way many enterprising nursing home residents and their families defeat this silent discrimination is to enter a better home while the senior still has sufficient assets to pay for their own care for a period of time. (Private-pay patients tend to find fewer waiting lines.) Then, when they run out of money, the home will assist them in obtaining Medicaid since they cannot be legally kicked out of the nursing home simply because they have run out of money and been forced onto Medicaid.

Preventing Involuntary Discharge

The law has come to recognize that unscrupulous nursing homes might try to get rid of residents who go on Medicaid or who assert their rights. As a result, laws have been created at the federal and state levels to prevent residents from suffering an unfair and unwarranted involuntary discharge. Specifically, residents cannot be discharged against their will unless:

- There are bona fide medical reasons, such as an extended hospitalization.
- The resident fails to pay their bill.
- It is necessary to protect the resident's welfare or that of other residents.
- The nursing home loses its Medicare or Medicaid certification.

Residents facing involuntary discharge also have procedural rights. For example, they have the right to be notified ahead of the discharge date of the action that the nursing home plans to take. Usually, this will be 30 days. There is also an appeal right, which is handled differently in every state. For more information, contact the nursing home administration or the Ombudsman's office.

If you wish to consult a lawyer about Medicaid planning, make sure the lawyer is intimately familiar with the ins and outs of "the system." You may wish to use a lawyer who is a member of the National Academy of Elder Law Attorneys. NAELA's administrative law office is located in Tucson, AZ. Its telephone number is (602) 881-4005.

CONSERVATORSHIPS

Conservatorships allow a relative, friend or other qualified person to be appointed by the probate court to manage the financial affairs and/or personal affairs of another who is unable to take care of these matters for themselves. There are two kinds of conservatorships. The "conservatorship of the estate" concerns the financial affairs of the needy person (known as the conservatee). A "conservatorship of the person" allows the conservator to make personal decisions for the conservatee, such as consenting to medical treatment and deciding where the conservatee shall reside.

Conservatorships are usually necessary when there are significant assets which the older person can no longer manage. The process is begun by filing a petition for conservatorship in court. At that point, the court will appoint the social welfare department to conduct an investigation to determine whether the requested action is required. After the report is written and evidence presented in court, the court will sign an order creating the conservatorship it deemed is in the best interests of the person requiring care.

Once the conservatorship has been established, the court will periodically review the case to ensure that the conservator is handling the affairs of the conservatee in a proper manner. The court will also be available to approve proposed decisions by the conservator if the matter might be controversial. For example, if a conservator believes it is in the conservatee's best interest to have extraordinary medical care removed because death is imminent, he or she might have to request the court for approval of the decision before the doctors will agree to take the requested action.

Conservatorships are court matters and the conservator has specific legal duties that should be understood before the responsibility to make decisions for another is accepted. Thus, it is a good idea to discuss the matter with an attorney before applying to the court to establish a conservatorship.

CONCLUSION

This book has sought to empower the reader by discussing some of the most compelling issues that face families today. Whether in the area of troubled families, divorce law, insurance or caring for aging parents, this book has sought to inform and enlighten, in the hopes that not only will readers be provided an interesting read but that they will be able to actively utilize what they have learned here to improve their family life.

APPENDICES

A STATE-BY-STATE GUIDE TO FAULT AND NO-FAULT STATES; LAWS OF PROPERTY DIVISION; RESIDENCY REQUIREMENTS

All states permit some form of "no-fault" divorce. Some states such as New York, New Jersey and North Carolina, are restrictive in their laws, limiting no-fault to such cases as where there has been a previous judicial separation, where the parties have been living separate for a specified time, or where the parties have a mutual consent decree (a decision about all of the issues involved in the divorce that's reached by the parties themselves and approved by the court). Most states, however, make it easy to obtain a divorce through the "irreconcilable differences" type of standard. The minimum residency requirement needed to obtain a divorce in each state is also listed.

The source for the following information is *The Family Law Quarterly*, Vol. 26, #4, American Bar Association. Chicago, IL. Winter 1993.

ALABAMA
Alabama permits most forms of no-fault divorce, as well as fault divorces. It is a separate property state. You must have lived in Alabama for six months to obtain a divorce.

ALASKA
Alaska does not permit irreconcilable differences type no-fault divorces but does permit incompatibility divorces and mutual consent decrees, as well as fault divorces. It is a separate property state. There is no time limit on the residency requirement but you must be a bona fide resident to obtain an Alaska divorce.

ARIZONA
Arizona permits irreconcilable differences type no-fault divorces and mutual consent decrees. Fault divorces are not permitted. It is a community property state. You must have lived in Arizona for 90 days to obtain a divorce.

ARKANSAS
Arkansas permits a no-fault divorce for having lived separate and apart for three years, as well as fault divorces. It is a separate property state. You must have lived in Arkansas for 60 days to obtain a divorce.

CALIFORNIA
California permits only irreconcilable differences type no-fault divorces and mutual consent decrees. It is a community property state. You must have lived in California for six months to obtain a divorce.

COLORADO
Colorado permits irreconcilable differences no-fault divorces and mutual consent decrees. Fault divorces are not permitted. It is a separate property state. You must have lived in Colorado for 90 days to obtain a divorce.

CONNECTICUT
Connecticut allows most forms of no-fault divorce, including living separate and apart and irreconcilable differences, as well as fault divorces. It is a separate property state. You must have lived in Connecticut for 12 months to obtain a divorce.

DELAWARE
Delaware allows irreconcilable differences and incompatibility forms of no-fault divorce, as well as fault divorces. It is a separate property state. You must have lived in Delaware for six months to obtain a divorce.

DISTRICT OF COLUMBIA
The District of Columbia permits no-fault divorces based on six months of voluntary separation or one year living separate and apart, as well as fault divorces. It is a separate property jurisdiction. You must have lived in the District of Columbia for six months to obtain a divorce.

FLORIDA
Florida permits irreconcilable differences type no-fault divorces, as well as fault divorces. It is a separate property state. You must have lived in Florida for six months to obtain a divorce.

GEORGIA
Georgia permits irreconcilable differences type of no-fault divorces, as well as fault divorces. It is a separate property state. You must have lived in Georgia for six months to obtain a divorce.

HAWAII
Hawaii permits irreconcilable differences type no-fault divorces as well as divorces based upon living separate and apart and mutual consent decree. Fault divorces are not permitted. It is a separate property state. You must have lived in Hawaii for six months to obtain a divorce.

IDAHO
Idaho permits both fault and no-fault divorces based on irreconcilable differences or living separate and apart. It is a community property state. You must have lived in Idaho six weeks to obtain a divorce.

ILLINOIS
Illinois permits no-fault divorce if there has been an irretrievable breakdown in the marriage and living apart for two years. Mutual consent divorces are permitted if the parties have been living apart for six months; fault divorces are also permitted. It is a separate property state. You must have lived in Illinois for 90 days to obtain a divorce.

INDIANA
Indiana permits only irreconcilable differences type no-fault divorces. It is a separate property state. You must have lived in Indiana for six months to obtain a divorce.

IOWA
Iowa permits only irreconcilable differences type no-fault divorces. It is a separate property state. You must have lived in Iowa for one year to obtain a divorce.

KANSAS

Kansas allows incompatibility type no-fault divorces, as well as fault divorces. It is a separate property state. You must have lived in Kansas for 60 days to obtain a divorce.

KENTUCKY

Kentucky allows incompatibility type no-fault divorces, as well as fault divorces. It is a separate property state. You must have lived in Kentucky for 180 days to obtain a divorce.

LOUISIANA

Louisiana permits no-fault divorces based on living separate and apart for six months, as well as fault divorces. It is a community property state. You must have lived in Louisiana for one year to obtain a divorce.

MAINE

Maine permits no-fault divorces based on irreconcilable differences, as well as fault divorces. It is a separate property state. You must have lived in Maine for six months to obtain a divorce.

MARYLAND

Maryland permits no-fault divorces based on living separate and apart for one year, as well as fault divorces. It is a separate property state. You must have lived in Maryland for one year to obtain a divorce.

MASSACHUSETTS

Massachusetts permits no-fault divorce based on irreconcilable differences if the parties sign a marital settlement agreement, as well as fault divorces. It is a separate property state. You must have lived in Massachusetts for one year to obtain a divorce.

MICHIGAN

Michigan permits only irreconcilable differences type no-fault divorces. It is a separate property state. You must have lived in Michigan for six months to obtain a divorce, but if the breakdown of the marriage arose out of the state, one year.

MINNESOTA

Minnesota allows only no-fault divorce, either based on an irreconcilable differences type standard or living separate and apart for 180 days. It is a separate property state. You must have lived in Minnesota for 180 days to obtain a divorce.

MISSISSIPPI

Mississippi allows irreconcilable differences type no-fault divorces, as well as fault divorces. It is a separate property state. You must have lived in Mississippi for six months to obtain a divorce.

MISSOURI

Missouri allows irreconcilable differences type no-fault divorces, as well as fault divorces. It is a separate property state. You must have lived in Missouri for 90 days to obtain a divorce.

MONTANA

Montana permits only no-fault divorces, either based on an irreconcilable differences type standard or living separate and apart for 180 days. It is a separate property state. You must have lived in Montana for 90 days to obtain a divorce.

NEBRASKA

Nebraska permits only no-fault divorces based on an irreconcilable differences type standard. It is a separate property state. You must have lived in Nebraska for one year to obtain a divorce.

NEVADA

Nevada permits no-fault divorce based on incompatibility or living separate and apart for one year, as well as fault divorces. It is a community property state. You must have lived in Nevada for six weeks to obtain a divorce.

NEW HAMPSHIRE

New Hampshire allows no-fault divorce based on an irreconcilable differences type standard, as well as fault divorces. It is a separate property state. You must have lived in New Hampshire for one year to obtain a divorce.

NEW JERSEY

New Jersey permits no-fault divorce based on living separate and apart for 18 months, as well as fault divorces. It is a separate property state. You must have lived in New Jersey for one year to obtain a divorce.

NEW MEXICO

New Mexico allows no-fault divorce based on incompatibility, as well as fault divorces. It is a community property state. You must have lived in New Mexico for six months to obtain a divorce.

NEW YORK

New York permits no-fault divorce based on a previous judicial separation for one year or more, as well as fault divorces. It is a separate property state. You must have lived in New York for one year to obtain a divorce.

NORTH CAROLINA

North Carolina allows no-fault divorce based on living separate and apart for one year, as well as fault divorces. It is a separate property state. You must have lived in North Carolina for six months to obtain a divorce.

NORTH DAKOTA

North Dakota allows irreconcilable differences type no-fault divorces, as well as fault divorces. It is a separate property state. You must have lived in North Dakota for six months to obtain a divorce.

OHIO

Ohio allows no-fault divorce based on incompatibility and living separate and apart for one year and mutual consent decrees, as well as fault divorces. It is a separate property state. You must have lived in Ohio for six months to obtain a divorce.

OKLAHOMA

Oklahoma permits incompatibility type no-fault divorces, as well as fault divorces. It is a separate property state. You must have lived in Oklahoma for six months to obtain a divorce.

OREGON

Oregon permits only no-fault divorce, based either on an irreconcilable differences type standard or mutual consent. It is a separate property state. You must have lived in Oregon for six months to obtain a divorce.

PENNSYLVANIA

Pennsylvania permits no-fault based on irreconcilable differences or living separate and apart for two years, as well as fault divorces. It is a separate property state. You must have lived in Pennsylvania for six months to obtain a divorce.

RHODE ISLAND

Rhode Island allows no-fault divorce based on the irreconcilable differences standard or living separate and apart for three years, as well as fault divorces. It is a separate property state. You must have lived in Rhode Island for one year to obtain a divorce.

SOUTH CAROLINA

South Carolina permits no-fault divorce based on irreconcilable differences or living separate and apart for one year, as well as fault divorces. It is a separate property state. You must have lived in South Carolina for one year to obtain a divorce unless both parties live in the state, then it is three months.

TENNESSEE

Tennessee allows no-fault divorce based on an irreconcilable differences standard and living separate and apart for three years, as well as fault divorces. It is a separate property state. You must have lived in Tennessee for six months to obtain a divorce.

TEXAS

Texas permits no-fault divorce based on living separate and apart for three years, as well as fault divorces. It is a community property state. You must have lived in Texas for six months to obtain a divorce.

UTAH

Utah allows no-fault divorce based on irreconcilable differences or living separate and apart for three years, as well as fault divorce. It is a separate property state. You must have lived in Utah for 90 days to obtain a divorce.

VERMONT

Vermont allows no-fault divorce based on living separate and apart for six months, as well as fault divorces. It is a separate property state. You must have lived in Vermont for six months to obtain a divorce.

VIRGINIA

Virginia permits no-fault divorce based on living separate and apart for six months, as well as fault divorces. It is a separate property state. You must have lived in Virginia for six months to obtain a divorce.

WASHINGTON

Washington permits only no-fault divorce, either based on an irreconcilable differences type standard or mutual consent. It is a community property state. There is no time requirement for residency but divorce is only available to those who truly reside in the state.

WEST VIRGINIA

West Virginia permits no-fault divorces based on an irreconcilable differences type standard or living separate and apart for one year. It is a separate property state. You must have lived in West Virginia for one year to obtain a divorce.

WISCONSIN

Wisconsin permits only no-fault divorce based on an irreconcilable differences type standard or mutual consent. It is a separate property state. You must have lived in Wisconsin for six months to obtain a divorce.

WYOMING

Wyoming allows no-fault divorce based on an irreconcilable differences type standard, as well as fault divorces. It is a separate property state. You must have lived in Wyoming for 60 days to obtain a divorce.

STATE CHILD SUPPORT ENFORCEMENT OFFICES

State Child Support Enforcement Offices are available to help: find absent parents, establish paternity (the biological father) of children, enforce legal support orders and collect child support payments. State offices can also put you in touch with local support enforcement offices.

The following list was compiled by the U.S. Department of Health and Human Services.

ALABAMA
Child Support Enforcement
   Division
Dept. of Human Resources
50 Ripley St.
Montgomery, AL 36130
(205) 242-3900

ALASKA
Child Support Enforcement
   Division
Dept. of Revenue
550 W. 7th Ave., 4th Fl.
Anchorage, AK 99501
(907) 276-3441

ARIZONA
Child Support Enforcement
Administration
Dept. of Economic Security
2222 W. Encanto
P.O. Box 40458 - Site Code 776A
Phoenix, AZ 85067
(602) 252-0236

ARKANSAS
Division of Child Support
   Enforcement
Arkansas Social Services
P.O. Box 3358
Little Rock, AR 72203
(501) 682-8398

CALIFORNIA
Child Support Program
   Management Branch
Dept. of Social Services
744 P St., Mail Stop 9-011
Sacramento, CA 95814
(916) 654-1556

COLORADO
Division of Child Support
   Enforcement
Dept. of Social Services
1575 Sherman St.
Denver, CO 80203-1714
(303) 866-5994

CONNECTICUT
Bureau of Child Support
   Enforcement
Dept. of Human Resources
1049 Asylum Ave.
Hartford, CT 06105
(203) 566-3053

DELAWARE
Division of Child Support
   Enforcement
Dept. of Health and Social Services
P.O. Box 904
New Castle, DE 19720
(302) 421-8300

DISTRICT OF COLUMBIA
Office of Paternity and
   Child Support
Dept. of Human Services
425 I St., NW, 3rd Fl.
Washington, DC 20001
(202) 724-5610

FLORIDA
Office of Child Support
   Enforcement
Dept. of Health and Rehabilitative
   Services
1317 Winewood Blvd., Bldg. 3
Tallahassee, FL 32399-0700
(904) 488-9900

GEORGIA
Office of Child Support Recovery
State Dept. of Human Resources
878 Peachtree St., NE, Rm. 529
Atlanta, GA 30309
(404) 894-4119

HAWAII
Child Support Enforcement
   Agency
Dept. of the Attorney General
680 Iwilei Rd., Ste. 490
Honolulu, HI 96817
(808) 587-3712

IDAHO
Bureau of Child Support
   Enforcement
Dept. of Health and Welfare
450 W. State St.
Towers Bldg., 5th Fl.
Boise, ID 83720
(208) 334-5710

ILLINOIS
Division of Child Support
   Enforcement
Dept. of Public Aid
Prescott E. Bloom Bldg.
201 S. Grand Ave., E.
P.O. Box 19405
Springfield, IL 62794-9405
(217) 782-1366

INDIANA
Child Support Enforcement
   Division
Dept. of Public Welfare
402 W. Washington St., Rm. W360
Indianapolis, IN 46204
(317) 232-4894

IOWA
Bureau of Collections
Iowa Dept. of Human Services
Hoover Bldg., 5th Fl.
Des Moines, IA 50319
(515) 281-5580

KANSAS
Child Support Enforcement
  Program
Dept. of Social and Rehabilitation
  Services
Biddle Bldg., 300 S.W. Oakley St.
P.O. Box 497
Topeka, KS 66603
(913) 296-3237

KENTUCKY
Division of Child Support
  Enforcement
Dept. of Social Insurance
Cabinet for Human Resources
275 E. Main St., 6th Fl. East
Frankfort, KY 40621
(502) 564-2285

LOUISIANA
Support Enforcement Services
Dept. of Social Services
P.O. Box 94065
Baton Rouge, LA 70804
(504) 342-4780

MAINE
Support Enforcement and
  Recovery
Dept. of Human Services
State House, Station 11
Augusta, ME 04333
(207) 289-2886

MARYLAND
Child Support Enforcement
  Administration
Dept. of Human Resources
311 W. Saratoga St.
Baltimore, MD 21201
(401) 333-3979

MASSACHUSETTS
Child Support Enforcement
  Division
Dept. of Revenue
141 Portland St.
Cambridge, MA 02139
(617) 621-4200

MICHIGAN
Office of Child Support
Dept. of Social Services
235 S. Grand Ave., Ste. 1046
P.O. Box 30037
Lansing, MI 48909
(517) 373-7570

MINNESOTA
Office of Child Support
  Enforcement
Dept. of Human Services
444 Lafayette Rd., 4th Fl.
St. Paul, MN 55155-3846
(612) 296-2499

MISSISSIPPI
Division of Child Support
  Enforcement
Dept. of Social Services
P.O. Box 1527
Jefferson City, MO 65102-1527
(314) 751-4301

MONTANA
Child Support Enforcement
  Division
Dept. of Social and Rehabilitation
  Services
P.O. Box 5955
Helena, MT 59604
(406) 444-4614

NEBRASKA
Child Support Enforcement Office
Dept. of Social Services
P.O. Box 95026
Lincoln, NE 68509
(402) 471-9125

NEVADA
Child Support Enforcement
    Program
Dept. of Human Resources
2527 N. Carson St., Capital
    Complex
Carson City, NV 89710
(702) 885-4744

NEW HAMPSHIRE
Child Support Enforcement
    Services
Division of Human Services
Health and Welfare Bldg.
6 Hazen Dr.
Concord, NH 03301
(603) 271-4426

NEW JERSEY
Division of Economic Assistance
Dept. of Human Services
Bureau of Child Support and
    Paternity Programs
CN 716
Trenton, NJ 08626
(609) 588-2361

NEW MEXICO
Child Support Enforcement
    Division
Dept. of Human Services
P.O. Box 25109
Santa Fe, NM 87504
(505) 827-7200

NEW YORK
Office of Child Support
    Enforcement
NY State Dept. of Social Services
P.O. Box 14 - 1 Commerce Plaza
Albany, NY 12260
(518) 474-9081

NORTH CAROLINA
Child Support Enforcement
    Section
Division of Social Services
Dept. of Human Resources
Anderson Plaza
100 E. Six Forks Rd.
Raleigh, NC 27609-7750
(919) 571-4120

NORTH DAKOTA
Child Support Enforcement
    Agency
Dept. of Human Services
P.O. Box 7190
Bismarck, ND 58507
(701) 224-3582

OHIO
Bureau of Child Support
Dept. of Human Services
State Office Tower, 27th Fl.
30 E. Broad St.
Columbus, OH 43266-0423
(614) 752-6561

OKLAHOMA
Child Support Enforcement
    Division
Dept. of Human Services
P.O. Box 25352
Oklahoma City, OK 73125
(405) 424-5871

OREGON
Recovery Services Section
Adult and Family Services Division
Dept. of Human Resources
P.O. Box 14506
Salem, OR 97309
(503) 378-5439

PENNSYLVANIA
Bureau of Child Support
  Enforcement
Dept. of Public Welfare
P.O. Box 8018
Harrisburg, PA 17105
(717) 787-3672

PUERTO RICO
Child Support Enforcement
  Program
Dept. of Social Services
CALL Box 3349
San Juan, PR 00902-3349
(809) 722-4731

RHODE ISLAND
Bureau of Family Support
Dept. of Human Services
77 Dorrance St.
Providence, RI 02903
(401) 277-2409

SOUTH CAROLINA
Child Support Enforcement
  Division
Dept. of Social Services
P.O. Box 1520
Columbia, SC 29202-9988
(803) 737-9938

SOUTH DAKOTA
Office of Child Support
  Enforcement
Dept. of Social Services
700 Governors Dr.
Pierre, SD 57501-2291
(605) 773-3641

TENNESSEE
Child Support Enforcement
  Division
Dept. of Human Services
Citizens Plaza Bldg., 12th Fl.
400 Deadrick St.
Nashville, TN 37219
(615) 741-1820

TEXAS
Child Support Enforcement
  Division
Office of the Attorney General
P.O. Box 12017
Austin, TX 78711-2017
(512) 463-2181

UTAH
Office of Recovery Services
Dept. of Social Services
120 N. 200 West
P.O. Box 45011
Salt Lake City, UT 84145-0011
(801) 538-4400

VERMONT
Child Support Division
Agency of Human Services
103 S. Main St.
Waterbury, VT 05676
(802) 241-2319

VIRGIN ISLANDS
Paternity and Child Support
   Division
Dept. of Justice
48 B-50 C Kronprindsens Gade
GERS Complex, 2nd Fl.
St. Thomas, VI 00802
(809) 774-5666

VIRGINIA
Division of Support Enforcement
   Program
Dept. of Social Services
8007 Discovery Dr.
Richmond, VA 23288
(804) 662-9962

WASHINGTON
Revenue Division
Dept. of Social and Health Services
P.O. Box 9162, Mail Stop HJ-31
Olympia, WA 98507
(206) 459-6481

WEST VIRGINIA
Child Advocate Office
Dept. of Human Services
State Capitol Complex
Bldg. 6, Rm. 812
Charleston, WV 25305
(304) 348-3780

WISCONSIN
Division of Economic Support
Bureau of Child Support
1 W. Wilson St., Rm. 382
P.O. Box 7935
Madison, WI 53707-7935
(608) 266-1175

WYOMING
Child Support Enforcement
   Section
Dept. of Health and Social Services
Hathaway Bldg.
Cheyenne, WY 82002
(307) 777-7892

GLOSSARY

ABANDONMENT Failure, on a continuous basis, to provide financial support and/or to communicate with a spouse or child.

ADOPTION A legal proceeding brought in court to create a parent-child relationship under the law between the adopting parent(s) and adopted child.

ADULTERY The sexual intercourse of a married individual with someone other than his or her spouse.

AGENT Someone who is legally allowed to act on behalf of another.

ALIMONY Court ordered payment for the financial support of an estranged spouse; used in the case of *divorce* or *legal separation.*

ANNULMENT A court order declaring that a marriage never legally existed.

APPEAL Request that a higher court review the decision of a lower court to correct errors in the application of law or procedure.

ARBITRATION Method of settling disputes in which the two sides submit arguments to a neutral third party or panel, which makes a decision after listening to both sides and considering the evidence.

ARREARS An amount of money owed that is overdue and unpaid.

ATTORNEY IN FACT The person appointed in a *durable power of attorney* to make health-care decisions on behalf of another.

BENEFICIARY A person to whom an insurance policy or the property from a *will* is payable.

COHABITATATION Living with someone in an intimate relationship without being legally married.

CLOSING Formal meeting of all those involved in the sale of real estate to exchange documents and money and execute the final deal.

COMMUNITY PROPERTY Property acquired during marriage that was not a gift to or inheritance of one spouse or specifically kept separate.

CONSERVATORSHIP   An agreement which allows a relative, friend or other qualified person to be appointed, by a judge, to manage the financial and/or personal affairs of someone who is incapacitated.

CONSIDERATION   The primary reason for a person making a *contract;* something of value received or promised to convince a person to make a deal.

CONTRACT   Binding agreement between two parties who have willingly exchanged something of value, called the *consideration.*

CUSTODY   A general term to show that an object or an individual is in the care and keeping of someone with legal authority. *Legal custody* occurs when one (or both parents in the case of joint legal custody) is allowed to make decisions about their child's education, health, and general welfare. *Physical custody* occurs when one (or both parents in the case of joint physical custody) is given physical control over their child.

DECREE   The decision or judgment of a court; an order having the force of law.

DEED   Formal representation of ownership of a piece of property.

DEFENDANT   Person against whom a legal action is filed.

DEPOSITION   Out-of-court process of taking the sworn testimony of a witness. This is done with a lawyer from the other side being permitted to attend or participate. The purpose is to disclose relevant information so that each side can evaluate its case before going to trial and decide whether to pursue the claim or settle out of court.

DISCOVERY   Before-trial formal and informal exchange of information between the sides of a lawsuit. Two types of discovery are *interrogatories* and *depositions.*

DIVORCE   A legal judgment that severs the marriage of two people and restores them to the status of single persons.

DURESS   Unlawful pressure or threats of violence which force a person to do things he or she might not otherwise do.

EMANCIPATED   To be set free. For example, a child is emancipated from his or her parents when he or she moves out, gets married or reaches legal age, leaving parents with no further right to control or obligation to support the child.

ESCROW   Money placed in a separate account to be used in previously agreed-to circumstances and released when certain conditions are met. Escrow money is often used in the transfer of property from one person to another.

ESTATE   All property that a person owns.

ESTATE PLANNING   Legal steps taken to transfer property after death or to reduce probate and tax costs.

FELONY   A serious crime, punishable with a long jail sentence and or death.

FIDUCIARY   Person in a position of trust and confidence; a person who has a duty to act primarily for the benefit of another.

GARNISHMENT   Legal proceedings in which a person's wages, property, money or credits are taken to satisfy payment of a debt or court judgment.

HEIR   Person designated to inherit property from someone who has died.

HOSPICE CARE   The treatment of terminally ill patients that concentrates on providing pain control and comfort rather than on curative methods.

INJUNCTION   A formal order from a judge to a person to do or to refrain from doing a particular thing.

INTERROGATORY   Form of *discovery* in which written questions posed by one side in a lawsuit require written responses under oath by the other.

JURISDICTION   A court's power to hear and determine a case.

JOINT TENANCY (with right of survivorship)   Form of ownership in which property is equally shared by all owners and is automatically transferred to the surviving owners when one of them dies.

LEGAL SEPARATION   A legal lawsuit for support while the spouses are living separate and apart. A legal separation may deal with the same issues as in a divorce, but does not dissolve the marriage.

LIEN   Legal claim to hold or sell property as security for a debt.

LIVING WILL   A document in which a person, while competent to do so, expresses a wish that his or her life not be prolonged by artificial life support systems if his or her medical condition becomes hopeless.

MARITAL PROPERTY   Property that has been acquired by either spouse during a marriage but owned equally by both, regardless of who holds title or whose earnings were used to obtain the property.

MEDIATION   Informal alternative to suing in which both sides to a dispute meet with a neutral third party (mediator) to negotiate a resolution. The resolution is usually put into a written agreement that is signed by both sides.

MISDEMEANOR   A criminal offense that is less than a *felony* and is punishable by a fine or a short jail sentence.

MORTGAGE   Formal document a home buyer signs pledging the property as security for the payment of a loan taken out to buy it.

MOTION   Request that a judge take specific action. For example, a "motion to dismiss" is a request that the judge throw a case out of court.

MUTUAL CONSENT DECREE   A decision about the issues involved in a divorce that is reached by the divorcing couple and approved by the court.

PATERNITY SUIT   A lawsuit that is initiated to determine who is the biological father of a child born out of wedlock.

PENSION   A fund or payments set up by an employer to pay employees after retirement.

PETITIONER   The person who intitates a lawsuit by filing a petition with the court.

PREMARITAL AGREEMENT   A contract between people planning to marry that establishes the rights and responsibilities each will have in the marriage and what will happen should one die or the marriage end in divorce. (Also known as antenuptial or prenuptial agreement.)

PROBATE   Legal process of establishing the validity of a deceased person's last *will* and testament; commonly refers to the process and laws for settling an *estate*.

PUNITIVE DAMAGES   Money awarded to a person who has suffered malicious and willful harm from another person. This money is not related to the actual cost of damages but serves as a warning against such an event happening again.

RESCIND   To cancel a contract as if it had never been.

SEPARATE PROPERTY   Where both spouses, the husband and the wife, enjoy sole ownership of property that is held in their individual name—even if the property is obtained during the marriage.

SETTLEMENT   An agreement about the final disposition of a lawsuit, including payment of debts, costs and so forth.

TENANCY BY THE ENTIRETY   Form of spousal ownership in which property is equally shared and automatically transferred to the surviving spouse. While both spouses are living, ownership of the property can be altered only by divorce or mutual agreement.

TENANCY IN COMMON   Way of jointly owning property in which each person's share passes to his or her heirs or beneficiaries, but the ownership shares need not be equal.

TITLE   Official representation of ownership that is transferred when a home is sold. Title can be "held" in the name of one or more persons.

TRUST   Property held by one party for the benefit of another.

VISITATION   The right of a parent who does not have *physical custody* to visit a child or have a child visit him or her.

WILL   Legal document that declares how a person wishes property to be distributed to *heirs* or *beneficiaries* after death.

WRIT OF EXECUTION   A court order or judgment which specifies a specific plan of action.

BIBLIOGRAPHY

The following books, some of which were used in researching this book, cover issues of concern to families. Some books listed may be out of print but should be available at your local library.

Divorce and Money: Everything You Need To Know About Dividing Property, by Violet Woodhouse and Victoria Felton-Collins, with M.C. Blakeman. Nolo Press, 950 Parker St., Berkeley, CA 94710. 1992. 288 pages. $19.95.

Describes, in plain language, the financial realities of divorce, the emotional impact and its effect on reaching a settlement, how to go from "we" to "me" and the important issue of what happens to the house.

Divorce Yourself: The National No-Fault Divorce Kit, by Daniel Sitarz. Nova Publishing Co., 4882 Kellogg Cir., Boulder, CO 80303. 1991. 331 pages. $24.95.

Provides information and instruction on how to obtain a no-fault divorce without using a lawyer. A state-by-state description of laws, such as residency requirements, legal grounds for divorce or dissolution and the availability of simplified divorce procedures for short-term marriages is also included.

Elder Care: Choosing & Financing Long-Term Care, by Joseph Mathews. Nolo Press, 950 Parker St., Berkeley, CA 94710. 1991. 224 pages. $16.95.

Focuses on issues relevant to families facing the prospect of paying for long term-care. Topics included are: care in the home, nursing homes, retirement communities and paying for it all.

Family Law Dictionary: Marriage, Divorce, Children & Living Together, by Robin D. Leonard and Stephen R. Elias. Nolo Press, 950 Parker St., Berkeley, CA 94710. 1988. 191 pages. $13.95.

Legal terminology is demystified in this valuable book which defines the words and phrases commonly used in domestic relations court and by family lawyers.

The Family Legal Companion, by Thomas Hauser. Allworth Press, 10 E. 23rd St., New York, NY 10010. 1992. 253 pages. $16.95.

Answers many of the most commonly asked legal questions in areas ranging from consumer rights, to divorce, to banking and credit, to travel, pets and insurance.

Funerals: Consumers' Last Rights, by the Editors of Consumer Reports. Consumers Union, 101 Truman Ave., Yonkers, NY 10703. 1977. 239 pages. (Out-of-print).

Even though written more than 15 years ago, this book contains all the consumer advice you will ever need about planning a funeral. From the people who bring you Consumer Reports magazine.

Home-Made Money: Consumer's Guide to Home Equity Conversion, American Association of Retired Persons, 601 E St., N.W., Washington D.C. 20049. 1991. 47 pages. Free.

Includes descriptions of different types of home equity conversions with an emphasis on reverse mortgages designed to help older Americans who are "house rich" but "cash poor."

How to Use Trusts to Avoid Probate & Taxes: A Guide to Living, Martial, Support, Charitable and Insurance Trusts, by Theresa Meehan Rudy, Kay Ostberg and Jean Dimeo in Association with HALT. Random House, 201 E. 50th St., New York, NY 10022. 1992. 231 pages. $10.00.

As the title suggests, this book provides a complete overview of trusts. Information on "living" and "testamentary" trusts, the pros and cons of each and how to get a trust drafted. State-by-state appendices, tax charts and glossary included.

Legal Rights for Seniors: A Guide to Health Care, Income Benefits and Senior Legal Services, by Wesley J. Smith. HALT—An Organization of Americans for Legal Reform, 1319 F St., NW, Ste. 300, Washington, D.C. 20004. 1993. 215 pages. $10.00.

Explains everything senior citizens and their families need to know about collecting important benefits and asserting their legal rights. Topics include, Medicare, Medicaid and Supplemental Security Income, living wills, pensions, estate planning and trusts, Veteran's benefits and nursing homes.

Life After Debt: The Blue Print for Surviving in America's Credit Society, by Benjamin F. Dover. Equitable Media Services, P.O. Box 9822, Fort Worth, TX 76147-2822. 1993. 307 pages. $16.95.

Gives tips on dealing with debt and provides sample letters and other forms for dealing with credit bureaus, banks and creditors.

The Living Together Kit, by Toni Ihara and Ralph Warner. Nolo Press, 950 Parker St., Berkeley, CA 94710. 1988. 240 pages. $17.95.

Describes the legalities of living together, including the issues surrounding unmarried sex, practical aspects of living together, living together contracts, buying a home, having children and what happens when an unmarried couple breaks up.

Probate: Settling an Estate: A Step-by-Step Guide, by Kay Ostberg in Association with HALT. Random House, 201 E. 50th St., New York, NY 10022. 1990. 162 pages. $8.95.

A "how-to" book for handling probate from start to finish. Includes a list of probate rules and death tax rates for each state and a check list of the tasks that need to be done.

Real Estate: The Legal Side to Buying a House, Condo or Co-op: A Step-by-Step Guide, by George Milko in Association with HALT. Random House, 201 E. 50th St., New York, NY 10022. 1990. 165 pages. $8.95.

Guides anyone through the process of buying a house or condominium. Among the topics covered are: evaluating areas and home prices, working with a real estate agent, making the offer and closing the deal, understanding the contract and how to shop for a mortgage.

The Senior Citizens Handbook: A Nuts And Bolts Guide to More Comfortable Living, by Wesley J. Smith. Price Stern Sloan Publishers, 11150 Olympic Blvd., Ste. 650, Los Angeles, CA 90064. 1989. 213 pages. (Out-of-print.)

This large-print book covers topics such as retirement living, avoiding scams, earning income, widowhood and health care. Introduction by Ralph Nader.

Where to Look for Help With a Pension Problem, Pension Rights Center, 918 16th St., N.W., Ste. 704, Washington, D.C. 20006. 1993. 43 pages. $8.75.

Lists government agencies and private organizations that answer pension questions, as well as legal programs that provide referrals and assist in pension cases.

Wills: A Do-It-Yourself Guide, by Theresa Meehan Rudy and Jean Dimeo. HALT—An Organization of Americans for Legal Reform, 1319 F St., N.W., Ste. 300, Washington, D.C. 20004. 1992. 254 pages. $8.95.

Gives advice about what you can give away in a will and how to prepare a will. Sample will clauses and a listing of state laws governing wills included.

Winning the Insurance Game: The Complete Consumer's Guide to Saving Money, by Ralph Nader and Wesley J. Smith. Doubleday Books, 1540 Broadway, New York, NY 10036. 1993. 538 pages. $14.95.

Describes life, health, auto, homeowner's insurance, as well as Medicare and Medicaid, and provides tips on successfully pursuing claims.

A Woman's Legal Guide to Separation & Divorce In All 50 States, by Norma Harwood, J.D. Charles Scribner's Sons, 115 5th St., New York, NY 10003. 1985. 330 pages. $11.95.

Although dated, this book provides a general description of the divorce law in all 50 states as it affects women. A valuable introduction to divorce law for those contemplating or going through divorce.

You Don't Always Need a Lawyer, by Craig Kubey. Consumer Reports Books, 101 Truman Ave., Yonkers, NY 10703. 1991. 244 pages. $15.95.

Explains the various ADR methods, gives tips on making alternate dispute resolution successful and provides a section on determining whether to hire a lawyer.

NATIONAL ORGANIZATIONS

ABA Section on Dispute Resolution
1800 M St., NW
Washington, DC 20036
(202) 331-2258
Provides information and referrals to mediation and arbitration programs. Write for a referral to a private or court-sponsored divorce mediation program in your area.

National Adoption Center
1500 Walnut Street, Ste. 701
Philadelphia, PA 19102
(215) 735-9988
Provides information and assistance on issues concerning adoption.

National Association of Crime Victim Compensation Boards
P.O. Box 16003
Alexandria, VA 22302
(703) 370-2996
Offers financial assistance to victims of violence. For a referral to the compensation board in your state, contact the association.

National Housing Institute
439 Main St.
Orange, NJ 07050
(201) 678-3110
Supports tenants' groups nationwide and acts as a resource center for information on tenants' rights.

National Insurance Consumer Organization
121 N. Payne St.
Alexandria, VA 22314
(703) 549-8050
Educates consumers through their publications on how to save money when buying insurance. Conducts advocacy work to protect consumers' rights.

NOVA – National Organization for Victim Assistance
1757 Park Rd., NW
Washington, DC 20010
(202) 232-6682
(800) 879-6682 (crisis hotline for local referrals)
Provides direct assistance, operates a clearinghouse of information, and conducts advocacy work on behalf of victims of crime.

Parent Information Center
210 Carlton Terrace
Teaneck, NJ 07666
(201) 692-0898
Advocates for the education rights of handicapped children.

About the Author

Wesley J. Smith is an author, a consumer advocate and an attorney. He is the author of *Legal Rights for Seniors, The Lawyer Book, The Doctor Book,* and *The Senior Citizens' Handbook.* He has coauthored two books with Ralph Nader, *Winning the Insurance Game* and *The Frugal Shopper.* Smith and Nader's next collaboration is *Collision Course: The Truth About Airline Safety,* to be published in fall 1993. Smith is also a lecturer and media commentator, having appeared before community groups, professional associations and educational gatherings across the nation.

About HALT

HALT — An Organization of Americans for Legal Reform is a national, non-profit, non-partisan public-interest group of more than 75,000 members. It is dedicated to enabling all people to dispose of their legal affairs simply, affordably and equitably. HALT pursues an ambitious program to improve the quality, reduce the cost and increase the accessibility of the civil legal system.

HALT pursues advocacy at the state and federal levels. In particular, HALT supports:

- Reforming "unauthorized practice of law" (UPL) rules that forbid nonlawyers from handling even routine uncontested matters, limit consumers' options and make legal services unaffordable to many.
- Assuring consumer protection against incompetence and fraud by replacing lawyer self-regulation with public control and accountability in systems for disciplining lawyers and judges.
- Developing standardized do-it-yourself forms and simplified procedures for routine legal matters such as wills, uncontested divorces, trusts and simple bankruptcies.
- Creating pro-consumer alternatives to the tort system, such as alternative-compensation systems that guarantee swift and fair compensation for those injured.

To achieve its educational goals, HALT publishes Citizens Legal Manuals like this one and an "Everyday Law Series" of brief legal guides to increase consumers' ability to handle their own legal affairs and help them become better-informed users of legal services. Written in easy-to-understand language, these materials explain basic legal principles and procedures, including step-by-step "how-to" instructions.

HALT's quarterly publication, *The Legal Reformer,* is the only national periodical of legal reform news and analysis. It informs readers about major legal reform developments and what they can do to help.

HALT's activities are funded primarily through member contributions.